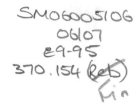

Pearson
PUBLISHING

Rebuilding Engagement through the Arts

Responding to disaffected students

John Finney, Richard Hickman, Morag Morrison,
Bill Nicholl and Jean Rudduck

D1439952

I believe in the powers of ordinary men and women; in their immense personalities; in their capacity to rise higher than themselves; in their essential creativeness; in them as artists. I do not believe in the 'chosen few'; I believe in us all.

Robin Tanner, teacher, artist and HMI; the quotation was featured at the centenary exhibition at Olympia, November 2004

Kids amaze me! They astonish me!

Secondary school teacher

Further copies of this publication may be obtained from:

Pearson Publishing
Chesterton Mill, French's Road, Cambridge CB4 3NP
Tel 01223 350555 Fax 01223 356484

Email info@pearson.co.uk Web site www.pearsonpublishing.co.uk

ISBN: 1 85749 858 5

Published by Pearson Publishing 2005
© Pearson Publishing 2005

Contents

Notes for readers

Acknowledgements

We would like to thank the Wallenberg Foundation for funding the project that enabled us to write the book. We recognise the generosity of the four schools in allowing us to work with them. Our thanks go also to the 11 students who took part and to their teachers and families who took an interest in their work and gave important encouragement. We were full of admiration for what the students achieved, for their organisational skills and for the quality of their insights into teaching and learning. We hope that their experiences as 'student teachers' will be something that they continue to look back on with pride.

About the book

Names – All names – of students, teachers and schools – have been changed. The sketches are based on photographs of the students involved but identifiable features have been eliminated.

Terminology – All the young people who took part from secondary schools are referred to as 'students'; the 11 students who are the main focus of the book are referred to as 'student teachers' when they are involved in their 'teaching episodes'. The young people from primary and infant schools who were involved are referred to as 'pupils' or 'children'.

Authorship – The work presented in this book was a team effort. All members of the team are from the Faculty of Education, University of Cambridge. John Finney, Richard Hickman, Morag Morrison and Bill Nicholl each took responsibility for working with students and teachers in one of the four participating schools and for writing their own 'story'. Jean Rudduck wrote Chapter 1 and was responsible for the overall editing; Jean, John and Morag wrote Chapter 6; John wrote Chapter 7. All five of us contributed to Chapter 8.

Other relevant publications

Other books from Pearson Publishing that explore the potential of pupil voice:

Arnot M, McIntyre D, Pedder D and Reay D (2003) *Consultation in the Classroom: Developing Dialogue about Teaching and Learning*

Fielding M and Bragg S (2003) *Students as Researchers: Making a Difference*

Macbeath J, Demetriou H, Rudduck J and Myers K (2003) *Consulting Pupils: A Toolkit for Teachers*

Rudduck J and Flutter J (2004) *The Challenge of Year 8: Sustaining Pupils' Engagement with Learning*

The project and the students

This book is about the ways in which young people who have disengaged from learning in school can find a way back through the arts. It tells the stories of 11 young people from four secondary schools who were able to use the talents they had in Art and Design, Design and Technology, Drama and Music – talents that were not always acknowledged within the formal curriculum – in ways that gave them a sense of self-worth and achievement.

The work was funded by a small grant from the Wallenberg Foundation and the research and development took place in 2003, with some follow-up events in 2004. Within a national and international context of active interest in young people's voice and participation, the project explored the potential of an approach to developing positive leadership qualities in students whose self-esteem as learners was low and who were not consistently committed to the school's learning purposes. Some also exercised a negative leadership role among their peers in school.

The stories are framed in three ways. First, they extend recent research on pupil voice and participation, exploring the possibilities of young people exchanging negative attitudes to learning and negative leadership roles for more positive ones. Second, they draw on the substantial body of work on peer tutoring: all the students involved were able to share their talents in formal teaching sessions with other pupils – sessions which they helped plan and which they led. Third, the project draws on contemporary research that points to the power of the arts in education to motivate young people and to enhance or rekindle their commitment.

The accounts enable us to see the changes in the students through the eyes of the students themselves and through the initially disbelieving eyes of some of their teachers.

The structure of the project

The four arts members of the team each chose the schools they wanted to work with and negotiated access. The link teacher in each school helped to identify some students in one of their Year 8 or Year 9 classes who s/he believed had talent in some aspect of the target subjects (Art and Design, Design and Technology, Drama or Music). For some students, this was the only subject they liked in school. Where they thought that teachers might well be unaware of some out-of-school talents, the researchers invited students in the classes to list their hobbies and skills. Seemingly relevant interests (such as drum-majoretting and graffiti art) were checked out by the researchers in discussion with the young people. Finally, between one and four students in each school were then invited to participate. The 'selection' was handled unobtrusively so that there was no sense among the others of having been rejected – an experience that could have weakened the already fragile commitment to learning of some students in the classes.

Profiles of the students involved were constructed from short interviews with the link teacher and with other teachers who taught them. We wanted to see how the students were perceived in different lessons and teachers were asked to comment on students' commitment to learning, self-esteem and standing within the peer group. The profiles constructed before the project started were checked against the comments made by teachers and students at the end of the project.

The students, the researcher and the link teacher then devised a classroom 'episode' or short unit of work that would allow the students to use their interests or skills to teach younger pupils or, in one case, students in the same year. When the teaching episodes were over, follow-up interviews were conducted with the target students – whom we called 'student teachers' – and with the students they 'taught'. For example, the following questions were used in the follow-up interviews with the target students in the art project.

Immediately after the teaching episode:
*   How do you think the lesson went?
*   Did the students learn?
*   How do you feel now you have completed the task?

Later:
*   Has it affected your role within your class or year group? How?
*   Do you think other students view you differently now?

Responses to the questions indicated, across the 11 students, greater self-esteem and the development of a more positive attitude towards teachers and school.

The 11 students

(All names have been changed; some students chose their own pseudonym.)

Ashley and Kayleigh, both in Year 8, were close friends. They were seen by their teachers as bright but disruptive, and as negative leaders in the sense that they were respected by their peers for their brash resistance. Drama was a subject they liked and their social confidence meant that they were often chosen to take part. For their teaching episode, they taught, together, a small group of Year 6s from the nearby primary school.

Lauren, in Year 8, was often on report and in detention for rudeness and disruption; she had a short fuse and often shouted at teachers. She had a reputation that went beyond her own year group for being naughty. However, like Ashley and Kayleigh, she usually behaved well in the lessons she did well in. Her mother had taught her to cook and in Food Technology classes in school she sometimes helped her slower or less competent peers. For her teaching episode, Lauren taught a small group of Year 7s.

Kurt and Graham had developed negative attitudes to school but were not overtly disruptive. **Graham** achieved well in some subjects but his tendency to boss others, coupled with his willingness to work hard in some lessons, turned him into a victim rather than a leader; he was beginning to be bullied and harassed, and was losing confidence. **Kurt's** sporadic attendance since he joined his secondary school made him worried about falling behind and he was trapped in a vicious circle. The greater his anxiety about keeping up, the less he wanted to come to school and the more he missed, the greater his anxiety became about falling behind. For their teaching episode, Kurt and Graham (both in Year 8) shared the teaching of a small group of Year 7s.

Mark and Jason were in Year 9. Both were talented in Art and Design but were generally difficult and disengaged. Jason was temporarily excluded during the early stage of the project but was followed up when he moved into Year 10. **Mark** had been described as 'gifted and talented' in Art and Design but in Year 9 his commitment to learning generally started to dip and he was known for instigating off-task activities, especially among his male peers. **Jason** had learning difficulties: his reading age was well below his chronological age, he was dyslexic and somewhat hard of hearing. Jason was often off-task in lessons, would challenge teachers and had generated an expectation among teachers and students that if there was 'an incident' he might well be involved. Mark taught part of a lesson to his own class while Jason taught his skills to others in a school club.

Tyson, Brian, Morgan and Rachel were all in Year 8 and all liked their Music lessons. **Tyson** had found the move to the big secondary school difficult; he was reluctant to accept authority and he could be disruptive. He liked to be the centre of attention and was looked up to by his peers, who were possibly rather afraid of him. Teachers judged him to be highly intelligent. **Brian** was seen by teachers as one of his year's 'Top 20 Troublemakers'. He was skilled in distracting others and goading them to misbehave. He was seen as strategically clever and – as the project interviews revealed – he had a good understanding of the social dynamics of school and classroom.

Morgan was the most recent in a long line of family members who had made 'bad tracks' at the school. She was seen as unmotivated, often off-task and subtly influential, using her anti-work stance as a way of maintaining authority over her peers. **Rachel** was argumentative and often involved in confrontations with the more overtly disruptive in her year group. She and Morgan together were seen as a potentially subversive pair. The four students worked together to teach a group of Year 7s.

Re-committing to learning

In earlier projects (Galton et al, 2003; Rudduck et al, 1996), we were interested in how tensions and pressures can lead students to adopt particular attitudes and persona in school and classroom and the difficulties they have in dropping them:

> It's all right saying 'Change' but you can't just stop like that, can you? **-Y10 boy**

Students who have adopted anti-work or anti-school persona can find it particularly difficult to change because their peers have certain expectations of them – as this student explains:

> I think trouble with me were when I come to school I messed about from day one so people got me as a mess-abouter from day one so like if I didn't mess about, 'Oh, you're boring'. You know what I mean? **-Y11 girl**

Students can also feel that their image and habits are held in place by their teachers – who have files and memories in which their behaviours and, indeed, their characters, are indelibly recorded:

> ... you mess around ... you get a reputation for yourself as a trouble-causer and you can't lose it – it's like there. **-Y11 boy**

Students understand what is at stake and are often surprisingly insightful and tolerant:

> Me personally I've brought a reputation upon myself. I'm known to be the class clown and that and it's got me in a lot of trouble. And so I've decided to change and it's just really hard to, like show the teachers that 'cos ... and then, like, I went on report, and I got, like, A1, A1, best, top marks. But there's been some lessons where it's slipped and they're [saying] like, 'Oh, he's still the same'. I can understand how they feel about that. **-Y10 boy**

It is not surprising that students like teachers who believe in 'a fresh start'.

Interviews from these earlier studies also suggested that when it gets to examination time students who had been, for whatever reasons, too laid back about work and/or who had regularly sought to disrupt the work of their classmates started to have some regrets. Interestingly, students mostly directed the blame to themselves – they also tended to see the situation as irredeemable:

> I were just running about like a little kid and not doing 'owt. I was really immature ... and then it were like [this year] it hit me ... I could have tried harder but can't turn back time. –Y11 girl

> I missed loads of school which was my own fault and I'm suffering from that now ... I thought, 'Oh it doesn't matter, I can make up the work' but I didn't. I don't know what we're doing so it's a waste of time now. –Y11 boy

Coping is difficult for those students whose self-confidence as learners and whose capacity to organise their lives effectively is fragile and some decide to opt out of the struggle:

> There's a few in our form that's settled down in the past year, that's got stuck into their work, but other people just don't care or don't bother coming to school. –Y10 girl

Teachers are often saying that they despair of trying to work with groups of students who have become what Chaplain (1996) called 'collaboratively disengaged' and who take heart in maintaining a noisy and extrovert disdain for schoolwork:

> If you fall into a bad group of friends then ... I know one group, their kind of mission is not to do well, to mess around, to get told off ... One of them is extremely clever and always does well but ... It's part of her group to act like that. –Y10 girl

Members of such groups do not find it easy to escape the pressure of the peer group. And change is not easy – even for those students who want to change. The triggers for change are different for different students. For some, the process of being asked to talk about problems in learning may in itself be a turning point and can help students rid themselves of the feeling that 'they don't listen to us'. For others, reassurance about their own capability can provide the trigger for change. They may be able to build a new confidence in themselves by being asked to take on a special role or responsibility, or by being able to use, in the classroom, skills and talents developed outside school that do not usually find a place in the routine curriculum. The process of disengagement can be reversed if students feel that significant others in the school are able to see and acknowledge some of their strengths.

In the project reported here, knowing that their skills had been recognised, being invited to do something special, and teaching a group of younger pupils were critical moments in the process of change.

We were aware of earlier studies (see Morrison et al, 2000) where similar 'transformations' had been recorded when disaffected students were given responsibility to mentor younger pupils. The additional dimension in our project was the central place of the arts.

The arts, peer teaching and engagement

We know that some students view the arts in school as an element of the curriculum that is different. They are quick to recognise the opportunity to negotiate personal space in learning and at the same time develop skills linked to particular art forms. A study carried out by the NFER (Harland et al, 2000) reported the sense of fulfilment in their own achievements that students said they experienced in their work in the arts, and also greater self-esteem. Such effects are also claimed by young people involved in the arts outside school.

A distinctive feature of the arts is the power to engage and sustain young people's interest and motivation. Where extrinsic motivation binds students into a task through the promise of praise or high grade or other reward, the arts are also strong on intrinsic motivation – the capacity to engage young people in an activity because it is interesting, involving, satisfying or personally challenging.

Csikszentmihalyi's description (1990) of 'flow experiences' emphasises similar things: where interest is strong, you have a sense that you are being taken along by the 'flow' of a river. Feelings of total absorption and deep enjoyment come from tasks that match people's interests and talents. These capture their curiosity and challenge them in ways they find exciting rather than daunting. This was the kind of experience we sought to offer the students who took part in our project.

The project started from the sure ground of students' own interests and talents but there was an added dimension – the possibility of sharing their skills with others. The benefits of managing a 'teaching episode' were twofold. First, teaching is an activity that involves both listening and being listened to; the disaffected or marginalised can expect to have a voice and for that voice to be heard. Second, there is the expectation that as 'teachers' they will have something valuable to offer to others. The role carries the promise of responsibility, recognition and respect. Maxine Greene (1995) underlines the importance, for young people who are in some way at risk, of developing a sense of self-worth and agency:

> … *young people are seldom looked upon as capable of imagining, or choosing… Instead, they are subjected to outside pressures, manipulations and predictions. The supporting structures that exist are not used to sustain a sense of agency among those they shelter: instead, they legitimate treatment, remediation, control – anything but difference and release.*

The project sought to give these young people release from the badges of identity that were constraining the development of alternative ways of relating and of achieving recognition. Peer teaching is a familiar way of reclaiming the confidence and commitment of young people whose difficulties with learning in school are expressed through disruption, disengagement or withdrawal. It builds on the recognised skills of the tutors – in our case the student teachers – and part of its success is the transforming power of feeling that what you have done matters.

Paul Willis (1992) wrote about the arts in the lives of young people, noting how the young are already 'culturally energised' and asking how in schools we might be able to tap into that energy. One response is to trust them more and to avoid underestimating them. When adults have high expectations of them, young people are more likely to use their skills in constructive ways. They also want, as our interviews repeatedly testify, more responsibility, more autonomy and to feel that they can make a difference. And young people can make a difference: it is important to forget the negative labels that we have stuck on them and that define them in narrow ways and instead to be alert to their 'unpredictable achievements'.

'I was, like, listened to and it made me feel proud'

It is around 4 pm at a local comprehensive school and the last lesson of the day is over. I had arranged to ring Ellen, the Drama teacher, and she answers the phone in her classroom.

I'm interested in working with some of your students, Ellen ... Negative leaders; kids who perhaps are a bit difficult; okay in Drama, but maybe not really behaving or focused in other subjects. Have you any ...?

She interrupts, 'Naughty kids. You want to work with some naughty kids?' I hear her call to the other teachers in the room, 'She wonders if we have some problem kids she can work with.' There is general hilarity in the background! She returns to the call, 'How many do you want?'

The school has an active Drama department, led by a very experienced teacher who is committed to the subject and to the students. When Ellen speaks about two young students, Ashley and Kayleigh, her no-nonsense description is underpinned by a great deal of warmth and you can sense immediately one of the reasons why these two students like Drama, despite their reputation as disruptive students in other subjects. They have been encouraged to believe that they have something to offer.

Difficult or challenging students tend to be attracted by Drama and it is often difficult to persuade colleagues in other subject areas that a nightmare student they may be dealing with in, say, Maths, is behaving well and working well in Drama. Ashley and Kayleigh are such students. They are seen as strong-willed but not always cooperative or focused in classes other than Drama. A teacher describes them:

They are both quite different ... they have a very big sort of face in the classroom if you like and will often lead quite disruptive behaviour, because other kids look up to them. They're well respected.

They appear to have an influential role among their peers, and it is hoped that this project might help them redirect their negative energy into something more positive. Ellen says that when she approached them to see if they would be interested in doing some peer teaching they became intrigued and agreed to an initial meeting the following Friday morning.

The two student teachers

One of Ashley's teachers, Anna, says of her:

Ashley is well respected because she is scary. You know, she can scare kids ... It's better to get on with Ashley than not get on with her.

Ashley is fourth in a family of five children, three of whom have been at this school, although none has so far made it to the end of Year 11. She seems to have difficulty concentrating and leads others astray in the classroom. She has a quick temper and an aggressive streak that has led her to instigate physical fights. According to one of her teachers, 'She wouldn't be able to talk her way out of anything, or reason with anybody. It would be fight first, talk later.'

Ashley is aware of her reputation and when asked to describe how she sees herself, she acknowledges that she is chatty in class, loud and 'mouthy'. Interestingly, she puts this down to the fact that she is a 'bubbly person', maintaining that the reason for her misbehaviour is because she has '... too much energy than what I need.' She thinks other people might well describe her as 'hyperactive', although this is not a description one hears from her teachers.

Despite Ashley's lack of focus in other subjects, she enjoys Drama and does well in the subject. In her own words:

You have to express everything. I just like it because I'm quite good at it and I like doing stuff that I know I can do fairly well. I like to show I have got confidence and stuff.

On the surface, it seems that Ashley's view of herself and her reputation in the school as an influential, albeit negative, leader would suggest a confident girl with a positive sense of self-worth. On meeting her, therefore, it is surprising to find her rather self-conscious. Indeed, as we work more closely together, it becomes apparent that her tough exterior might be just that – an external appearance. Perhaps for Ashley, acting a role is much easier than being Ashley.

A teacher whom Kayleigh has had since Year 7 describes her:

Kayleigh is funny because she's very bright, so you can have a good conversation with her. She can get rude though. I mean there are certain teachers that she will be rude to.

Kayleigh and Ashley are good friends. They have known each other since their primary years and socialise with each other outside school. As with Ashley, education has not been a high priority in Kayleigh's family. Kayleigh is described by Ellen as a bright girl but one hampered by a lack of commitment in class, often overly chatty and unfocused. A number of Kayleigh's teachers used the well-worn phrase 'Can do better' on her Year 8 reports and commented also on her regular absences from school. She is quite a strong personality within the school and looked up to by her peer group. Although not as volatile as her friend, she can be challenging. It seems that together these two girls are quite a handful.

Kayleigh enjoys Drama and is always eager to participate and contribute. Ellen, their Drama teacher, comments, 'Ashley and Kayleigh are good, particularly in role play; they are quite happy to show what they can do. They quite often get chosen.' Another teacher says, 'She's got a lot going for her, Kayleigh. But she's kicking the system a bit.'

As with Ashley, surface appearances can be deceptive and the experienced young woman who first presents may not be the whole story. Kayleigh herself says, 'I like to be different people and play different roles.' Outside school, Ashley and Kayleigh lead very adult lives. They have family responsibilities and social lives which include clubbing and partying with people older than themselves. In school, autonomy is limited – so it must seem to Ashley and Kayleigh that childhood is difficult to escape from. Both young women seek attention and respect, but in different ways. Despite their labels as leaders, neither feels she has any formal power at school. Kayleigh wants to be seen as an adult and projects an image which demands to be noticed, whilst Ashley uses challenging behaviour to test the boundaries.

Getting involved

The first phase of the project takes place over one term. The girls' teacher, Ellen, agreed to monitor, informally, any impact on their progress in school. Given her other commitments, Ellen's participation beyond that had to be low key. It was decided from the outset that Ashley and Kayleigh should have as much responsibility as possible for the shape of the peer-teaching project. They are asked what they want to teach as well as who they would like to teach and where. The girls are to be teachers, so they will take responsibility for planning and delivering the lessons. The staff at Blakefield are encouraging and we are invited to have our planning sessions in the school's special conference room. Ashley and Kayleigh have never been in the room before and are obviously impressed by their surroundings. They giggle as they sit close together on one side of the large teak table. They seem pleased to be selected to work on this peer teaching project and by the end of the first morning one can sense that it makes them feel rather special. They gradually begin to look more at home.

Ashley and Kayleigh talk first about which aspects of Drama they enjoy most and what they feel they could teach others. They think that how to play a role and how to act convincingly are important skills. Both girls are reluctant to teach their immediate peers but like the idea of working with a group of primary school pupils. Both have a reputation within the school and working outside it will give them an opportunity to reinvent themselves in a different context. It is also interesting that, despite their own behaviour patterns, Ashley and Kayleigh feel it is important that their pupils behave. They decide it might be easier to teach a small group, no more than ten pupils, and they want to team teach. 'Crowd control!' they say in unison. They opt for Year 6 pupils.

This is a lively meeting. They talk about the kinds of things they enjoy in Drama and what they feel will be appropriate to teach to a Year 6 group. Ashley emphasises the need to know something about the pupils:

> Perhaps if we spend a little bit of time with that group we could see what they were into and their hobbies and stuff – hang around with them.

Kayleigh thinks this may be tricky to arrange and suggests asking them directly, 'We could find out stuff about them; ask them what they do after school and everything.'

Both Ashley and Kayleigh are enthusiastic about the idea of asking questions that may help them to select the pupils they will work with. For example, Ashley says:

> I would like confident ones that are not going to be shy and will stand up and show their expressions. The quiet ones would be a challenge as well. It would be good to mix them in so you could, like, the quiet ones could learn from the confident ones and influence them. I mean place the confident ones with the quiet ones to help them to work together.

Interestingly, Ashley corrects herself in that statement: rather than stay with the term 'influence' she has chosen 'work together'. Collaboration is a recurring theme in discussions about how they will approach their teaching.

A great deal is revealed also about what Kayleigh sees as good practice when she describes how she will approach her pupils:

> I find it would be easier to work with them as well, rather than sit there and speak to them and, like, give them instructions.

The morning has been successful and so times for further meetings are arranged. So much to do: a primary school to visit, a questionnaire to write, the responses to read, lessons to plan. Ashley and Kayleigh have some hard work ahead but are looking forward to it. Ashley is confident and says, 'I can organise and I think I could, like, motivate, if you can say that word.' Kayleigh just smiles and says, 'It sounds exciting – a challenge.'

Taking responsibility

By the time of our next meeting, a primary school nearby has been chosen. The headteacher is happy for them to work with one of the Year 6 classes. Ashley and Kayleigh are invited to visit the school the following week and agree to try to have the questionnaires ready to distribute. They discuss what information is needed in order to select their group. They decide that there will be a few areas on the form where pupils can tick boxes but that, generally, the survey will require written responses. This means that their pupils will have a personal voice. Kayleigh suggests that we should end the survey with a question that directly asks the pupils to plot on a continuum how they rate their confidence.

Ashley and Kayleigh take the preparation of the survey very seriously and debate in detail the wording of the questions. Even though they have yet to meet their pupils, this initial activity is engaging them and giving them a sense of responsibility. They are looking forward to getting the responses back. Although they themselves have been on the receiving end of questions and tests many times, this will be the first time they have had any say in their construction.

Next week, Ashley and Kayleigh arrive in the foyer well in advance of the starting time. (This becomes a pattern. No matter how unreliable or tardy they may be for their lessons, they are always sitting in the reception area ready for their work as teachers – on the dot!) Back in the conference room, the completed questionnaires are divided up between the three of us and read carefully. Ashley and Kayleigh enjoy reading aloud any responses that amuse them and we start to get a real sense of the Year 6 mind!

The task of sorting and deciding is handled expertly. The girls know that they have two main things to look for – information about individuals and information that will give a general idea of the interests of most Y6 pupils.

Kayleigh begins to jot down notes about which films and books are most frequently mentioned. They pick up also on gender differences in responses and this prompts Ashley to comment that there should be an equal number of boys and girls in the group. The responses are reread, re-sorted, and a short list of girls and boys is placed in the middle of the table. Most of the pupils have little or no experience of doing Drama, but it is agreed that it is how keen they are to learn that is most important. Ashley and Kayleigh have already decided that they want a mixture of confident and less confident pupils, so Kayleigh's suggestion that they ask the Year 6s to plot their perceptions of themselves proves very valuable.

Again, it is striking to note how empowering this process is for Ashley and Kayleigh. They are not afraid to disagree with each other or with Ellen and me. They listen and justify their own ideas and interpretations. There is a real spirit of collaboration in the process. Finally, four boys and four girls are selected: the Drama class has its members.

The other major decision is what is to be explored in the Drama lesson. The responses suggest that these Year 6 students like spooky stories and mysteries, so that will form the basis for the work. Although it is obvious that Ashley and Kayleigh are more fond of Drama based on 'real life', they are true to their commitment to listen to Year 6 – so fantasy it will be.

After Ellen leaves to take another lesson, the idea of a final performance for the rest of Year 6 emerges. It is suggested that this may be too ambitious, because of lack of time, but the girls are adamant that if they write a short script for eight characters, they can use this as a basis for teaching acting skills. It is hard not to be a little sceptical, especially later when their teacher comments, 'Do you know how difficult it is to get *any* written work out of these students?'

Later that week, we meet Ashley and Kayleigh at the primary school and manage a quick look round the school. The head is very pleasant to the girls and, in the spirit of the project, invites them to come back with their diaries at lunchtime, so that he can discuss dates.

Throughout the following two weeks, Ashley and Kayleigh work hard on their script. They get together at night or talk over the phone and each is writing a different scene. They must have it finished for their first session with the Drama class. It is a Haunted House mystery, reminiscent of storylines from Scooby Doo cartoons, but without the dog! Six children go to spend the night in a deserted house and two of them go missing. The script will not win any literary awards, but it contains the ingredients Kayleigh and Ashley have identified as appealing to Year 6 students. It is also a major achievement in that the girls are actually writing it themselves.

As each scene is completed, they show their work for approval. Although they have not yet met their pupils, they have a fair idea of the mix of personalities they have selected. It is impressive to note that they have thought about characters that will suit each member of their Drama group. The roles of the parents are given to pupils who seem a little shy because they don't involve as much action, whereas the prankster characters go to the more confident pupils. The girls are also trying to ensure that the play has roughly equal speaking parts for each person. All these considerations show a sensitive concern about inclusion, though it is hard not to become concerned that, in their zeal, the play will be too long!

Although the planning process has been lengthy, it has been important. Before Ashley and Kayleigh even begin their teaching, they are being given responsibility, trust and autonomy. They are enjoying what they are doing and committing themselves to the project. They are growing enormously in confidence and taking their roles as teachers very seriously.

A letter is sent home to Ashley and Kayleigh's parents telling them what the girls are doing and praising the effort they have made so far. Apparently, letters rarely go home from the school that are not about their inappropriate behaviour, so this one is a novelty. Ashley says:

> Mum goes, like, 'What have you done wrong, Ashley?' and then she reads it out properly. So funny.

Although secretly pleased, neither girl is used to praise so they are also embarrassed. Kayleigh recounts what happened when her mother opened the letter:

> My Mum was like, all happy and that. Then she started showing it to all my family and that, and I'm like ... [groans].

Ashley and Kayleigh join me at the University for lunch one day, out of school uniform and dressed up for the event. There is much excitement. Despite the fact that this is a University town, girls like Ashley and Kayleigh are unlikely ever to see behind the walls of the Colleges. This world is completely alien to them and they seem in awe of everything. Their behaviour is impeccable, almost too polite; they are very self-conscious and there is a great deal of giggling over lunch. Everything about it impresses them – the grounds, the buildings, even the food! They seem surprised that many students actually live in this beautiful place, but when told that they could too, Ashley is sceptical. She wants to be an actress, so probably will need to go to a Drama school she says. Kayleigh, however, is interested in nursing, and when told that nurses study for a university degree she seems even more interested. On their return to school, on being asked how they enjoyed the visit, 'It was quality!' says Kayleigh.

Beginning to care

Arriving to take Ashley and Kayleigh across to the primary school on the morning of their first lesson, I find them already waiting, excitedly clutching the scripts and scribbled notes about the shape of the lesson. The play is complete, typed and copied. We track down a whiteboard marker so that they can jot down the learning 'targets', and all is ready to begin.

The lessons are to take place in the school's multipurpose gym/recreation hall – a new building, brightly curtained and with a polished wooden floor. Ashley and Kayleigh seem well aware of the potential hazards of the space though and (recognising the 'fun' that can be had in socks on a slippery floor and the temptation of the vaulting horse for climbing) decide that the class should be conducted with shoes on and as far as possible away from the gym equipment.

The allotted 45 minutes is to be squeezed in between a year assembly and morning break, so there is some concern when, after five minutes, the class has not arrived. Just as it seems an investigation of their whereabouts might be in order, there is a commotion in the hallway and seven giggling Year 6 students arrive. Ashley and Kayleigh bring them in to sit in a circle. The girls introduce themselves whilst the Year 6 group, on their very best behaviour, sit quietly. They all seem a bit bemused by the whole arrangement but each replies shyly when asked their name. When Kayleigh tells them she hopes they will all like learning about Drama so they can perform for their class, there is a ripple of mock dissent from the boys, so she addresses one of them directly, 'You really don't have to do this if you don't want to.' Blushing, the boy mumbles that it might be 'orright' and that he does want to stay.

Things liven up considerably when Kayleigh explains that, first of all, they will be playing a drama game. The two girls have selected their own favourite game, 'Keeper of Keys', as a warm-up activity. The class loves it and by the end of the game they are more lively. Energy is high as the class sit back in the circle and Ashley hands around the scripts. It is noticeable that she is taking a support role and letting Kayleigh do most of the talking. Kayleigh seems happy to take control. The girls had been planning to take turns in explaining each character, but Ashley looks to Kayleigh when struggling to articulate the ideas. The class then begins a read-through of the whole script.

There is just enough time left to begin talking through Scene One. This scene involves everyone except the parents, and it is suggested to Ashley that she could take this opportunity to work in another part of the room with those characters. She is far more confident with this smaller group and less self-conscious. She works very sensitively with them, encouraging them as they struggle to bring the lines to life. Kayleigh meanwhile is setting a cracking pace, already improvising the action in a playground scene with her group. The sophisticated level of questioning Kayleigh uses is impressive. Rather than suggest her own ideas, she asks the group for theirs, and seeks explanation from them where appropriate before deferring to their opinion. Kayleigh highlights concepts she wants them to learn and then reinforces an understanding with reminders, using the language of Drama, 'Don't forget to look at who you are speaking to. Use eye contact. Try to focus and stay in role,' she directs.

Kayleigh is very encouraging and supportive but she is also aware of the need to think ahead. When two of the boys are joking and fidgeting as they wait for their line, she recognises a potential floor wrestle and cleverly calls one boy up to enter the scene a little earlier than his line requires – he is now occupied and out of temptation's way.

When the bell goes, the two groups are quickly called back together. Kayleigh reinforces a couple of points she has made earlier about trying not to laugh when in role. 'That is called "focus",' she says, and points to one of the targets written on the whiteboard. The group is praised for how hard they have worked and told to look after their scripts. The beaming Year 6 pupils then leave. Ashley and Kayleigh breathe melodramatic sighs of relief but it is obvious that they have enjoyed themselves.

It has been amazing to see how maturely and expertly the girls handled the class and they are told this. Ellen has come over from the high school to hear how their first lesson went and they are full of information. They excitedly tell her about their class and what they already think of some of the Year 6 personalities.

Over the next two weeks, Ashley and Kayleigh have two more lessons with their Drama class but time will be tight. The Year 6 pupils are enjoying themselves but also seizing opportunities to muck about when they are not in a scene. They are also very concerned about the lack of props and find it difficult to 'imagine' them into being.

However, Kayleigh and Ashley are managing well. Ashley's confidence is growing and the two are very much teaching as a team by the end of the second lesson. They are united in their frustration with the naughty behaviour, but circumspect in any criticism. They discuss strategies and decide that props might be a good idea after all. They also think it may be helpful if Ashley is positioned offstage, so that she can keep an eye on potential troublemakers. When there is too much general misbehaviour, the group is brought together: a serious talk is needed. 'Do you want to do this performance?' Kayleigh asks with gravity. 'Well, read my lips. Everyone has to focus!'

It is amusing to hear her use one of Ellen's favourite expressions. However, the talk seems to work and by the end of the third lesson, some progress is being made. Ashley and Kayleigh are happy to exchange friendly banter with the group; they are having fun and there is much laughter, but the girls are also focused and firm.

Back at their own school, Ashley and Kayleigh's work is being discussed by their teachers and the girls are enjoying the positive attention. Kayleigh proudly says:

> Everybody keeps saying, 'Yeah, you behaved very well; we're all pleased that you are getting on really well' and like Miss Swithin keeps saying 'How is it going?'

There has also been encouraging informal feedback coming to Ellen about their behaviour in other classes; the girls seem more mature and settled. At one stage, their English teacher makes a point of saying that he can really see a difference in Ashley's behaviour.

Interestingly, the girls are keeping very low key about the project with their peers and are possibly embarrassed about the positive attention they are getting. As Kayleigh explains:

> We've spoken to like a couple of people that we can trust and they're just like going to keep it quiet 'cos you don't want the whole school knowing about it and like going 'Did you hear about Ashley and Kayleigh?' and that.

Under pressure

Because of mid-term break, there was an unfortunate gap of two weeks between the last lesson and this, the fourth Drama class at Meadowbank. This time, however, Ashley is waiting in the car park, but not Kayleigh. Ashley has tried to get her on her mobile but there has been no answer and it seems this lesson will have to be a solo effort. Ashley says she is a little nervous, but wants to do it; she is aware that it will be disappointing to the Year 6 group if we don't proceed. She says that Kayleigh has the notes about what they were to teach today, so she is not sure how to start the lesson. Ashley has seemingly relied very much on Kayleigh to lead things, and even though planning is meant to be done jointly, it is Kayleigh who has been the organiser. However, Ashley is not going to admit this and insists she will be fine on her own. To help her a little, I offer to take the group for a Drama game warm-up. She can then take over.

The Year 6 group seems pleased to see us again and asks after Kayleigh. Ashley tentatively tells them she will take them on her own today. A quick, active, warm-up activity is conducted and Ashley then calls them into a circle. In the intervening two weeks, some pupils have mislaid their scripts, so there is a hiatus in proceedings as we try to locate spare copies. There is also confusion about which point had been reached in the play at the end of the last lesson and Ashley becomes flustered. She is not decisive and the group are detecting this. Ashley pauses to think about what she should do next and then, more in a spirit of desperation than democracy, asks the group: 'Errmm, well, what should we do now? I can't think …' She is cut short by one of the boys, 'Well, *you're* the teacher!'

Ashley realises that the Drama group have sensed her insecurity and are going to test her. To her credit, she does not look for help or intervention. She is going to battle on. She takes some pupils to the other end of the room to rehearse one of the scenes. A number of them can't remember their stage directions. Meanwhile, pupils not in this scene are fooling around and Ashley is finding it difficult to give attention to both groups. The rehearsal is becoming disorganised and she is struggling to gain control. Finding it difficult to think on her feet, she is becoming increasingly flustered. The boys' off-task behaviour is escalating and when Ashley makes a half-hearted attempt to get them back to work, she is ignored. Although she has still not asked for rescue, it is painful to watch.

She struggles through to the end of the lesson, although little is achieved. One student pointedly asks if Kayleigh will be back for the next lesson and this question must have made her feel wretched. The lesson has not gone well. Ashley is well aware that she was not well prepared, nor in control. She has appeared vulnerable in front of the Year 6 group so her pride, an important thing for Ashley, is hurt.

After the lesson, Ashley says she knows she mucked up the lesson, that her mind had just gone blank and she forgot what she had to do. However, it is pointed out to her that, as we have two lessons this week, the students will find it easier to remember where they are up to and she can be more prepared next time. The next lesson will be solo for her again, for we have heard that Kayleigh has left for a family holiday and will not be here for the next lesson either. Ashley then leaves to go to her own Drama class. Later, Ellen will ask her how it went today, as she always does, and it will be hard for Ashley to tell her. Ellen says Ashley feels dreadful about it and is blaming herself for what went wrong but she believes that it isn't a disaster but will 'actually be a good thing'. She explains, 'Ashley cares that it went wrong. Ashley cares about something; the project must matter to her'.

Ellen elaborates:

> *If you start to care about something, that's actually quite dangerous. Because if you start to care how well you do, say at school, then if you fail it matters. Whereas if you spend all your time saying 'I don't care', then if you fail it doesn't matter.*

The question is, though, will Ashley turn up on Friday? The lesson will be a huge challenge. Will Ashley be brave enough to face it?

Meeting the challenge

On Friday morning, contrary to fears that Ashley will not be in the car park, there she is, already waiting. Told that it is very good to see her today after the tough time she had on Tuesday, she shrugs (a quick glimpse of the old Ashley nonchalance) then says earnestly that she has really thought about what happened and has to prove she can do it. We re-enter the lion's den.

Ashley is totally prepared today and has planned step by step what she wants to do. When the Year 6 group arrive in high spirits she does not smile or giggle, but ushers them into the room and immediately sets out the goals for today's lesson in a business-like fashion. The group is given no time to waste, so moves quickly from the Drama warm-up game into the rehearsal process. Ashley is totally in control and she makes it clear they have a lot of work to do if they are going to be ready for a performance next week.

The rehearsal goes well. If someone forgets a line, they laugh together, but Ashley ensures they are then straight back on task. If any of the boys even look like they are planning to misbehave, Ashley reminds them of what they have learned about focus and about responsibility to the group. At the end of the lesson, Ashley is genuinely proud of what she has achieved, particularly in the light of the previous lesson's fiasco.

On leaving, Ashley wants to talk about the lesson so we find a place to chat until lunchtime when it will be time to tell Ellen what has happened.

Ashley begins by saying how she felt on Tuesday:

> I was all nervous and I didn't feel very much in control of them.
> I felt sort of like an idiot. All these questions were racing through
> my head and I didn't know what to say. I was a bit frightened as
> well because I didn't want to muck up, but I did. So I felt gutted
> after Tuesday's lesson.

Ellen was right, Ashley did care about her performance:

> The project means a lot to me. I felt like I'd mucked up and I
> wanted to put it right and sort of prove myself. I wanted to
> prove something to myself that I can do this all by myself. It
> gives me the confidence I knew I had inside me. Today I thought
> I'm going to ... show what I can do. So I did. I felt so proud, I
> like sort of thought to myself 'You've done well; you've proved
> everyone wrong.' It made me so happy.

As well as needing to prove something to herself, she seems aware that there
is a bigger battle – proving herself to others:

> ... like when someone is loud and mouthy, they go, 'Oh, that's
> just Ashley' and I've like this reputation hanging over me and I
> don't really want it. I want to be looked at as me, not just
> my reputation.

These are big admissions for Ashley, the capable and caring Ashley. What she
has needed is the freedom to reveal that side of herself and this project has
given her that opportunity.

Feeling like teachers

The following week Kayleigh is back from holiday and she and Ashley
conduct the final rehearsal with the Year 6 Drama class. It is not certain
whether Ashley has told Kayleigh much about what happened the week
before, but Kayleigh is, as usual, quite calm. The Year 6 group is in a state of
excited panic – one final run-through before the audience arrives. Ashley is
more up to date with where the group is and with what scenes need the
most urgent work, so she is able to share leadership with Kayleigh in this
lesson. Ashley and Kayleigh stress, in no uncertain terms, that the group is to
remain 'focused and professional'.

It may not be the most polished performance ever staged, but the audience seems to like watching their peers perform. All things considered, the performance is a success and Ashley and Kayleigh leave Meadowbank for the last time feeling happy and relieved. I stay behind to have a few words with the Year 6 group about how they felt about their teachers:

> It was easy to learn from them because they were like helping us how to do things.

The Y6 group agrees that it was good being taught by Ashley and Kayleigh. They talk about the element of 'fun' that Ashley and Kayleigh have brought to learning:

> With a teacher you can't have a laugh. You can't have fun about doing it.

> I enjoyed it because if we done anything wrong they didn't shout at us.

When asked what they feel they have learned it is not surprising that the first response is a chorus of 'Focus!' with much laughter. Several remember that 'facial expression' and 'eye contact' were things they had to learn. One girl identifies a term and explains why it is important:

> Levels, they taught us like different sorts of, like, levels. So not all on the same level. So it can look more interesting.

Back at their school, Ashley and Kayleigh are very pleased with themselves. Despite Kayleigh's calm exterior throughout the sessions, she now admits it was a challenge for her too:

> It's not as easy as I thought. Like at the beginning of it I just think they thought it was messing about; they thought it were just a laugh. But they got really into it and most of them in the end went home and they learnt their words and that, you know what I mean.

Both girls also comment on the perspective they now have of what a teacher has to do and Ashley remarks, 'I've started to appreciate more sort of [pause] the teachers really.' We all recognise the irony in this and laugh. Kayleigh adds, 'Some of them have got the patience of a saint – no, they have!'

Ellen finds us talking in the Drama room and tells Ashley and Kayleigh that she has just picked up their latest reports. Her smile implies they will be pleased. Comments from other teachers suggest there has been an improvement in their attitude and behaviour – which seems to have coincided with their involvement in the peer teaching project. Comments on Ashley's reports include '… sound progress … particularly pleased with the improvement I have seen in her behaviour', '… a lot more settled', '…improved attitude to work'. Teachers have also reported a visible improvement in Kayleigh's behaviour and, although attendance is still an issue, her reports seem to indicate more engagement in school, '… good attitude and effort', '… marked improvement in skills', '… Kayleigh has worked on some tasks with great enthusiasm.'

There is evidence that the project has had a positive impact on the academic motivation of both girls, but the influence it has had on their personal and emotional development may also be important. Ashley tries to explain how the teaching made her feel:

> It makes you feel good. It makes you feel like you've gave something to someone and you haven't received nothing back, besides like proudness and that.

Kayleigh has obviously enjoyed the teaching too:

> I don't know, I felt more mature after I had done it, because I think it was the fact that I was teaching people. I don't know, it was weird.

Ashley's comments also include reference to a new sense of power – a realisation that she could be 'heard' in a positive way: 'I was, like, listened to and it made me feel proud.'

The following week, when I was in the staffroom talking to Ellen, another of the girls' teachers arrives. She describes a recent lesson where she overheard Ashley talking to her peers about a book she is reading:

> *She was reading bits of it out to others and she was talking about how emotional it made her feel, which I don't think she would have talked about before. I think she has made a huge journey in a short time.*

Another of Ashley and Kayleigh's teachers says:

> *I think it is sad that we judge kids by the written exam and not what they can do. I think there should be more opportunities to value the creative side too. The system says they have to pass exams … that only means how well they write.*

Peer teaching is challenging because it requires responsibility and confidence. The project fostered emotional engagement and gave Ashley and Kayleigh the opportunity to stretch themselves as leaders. Teaching others requires active problem-solving and risk-taking – skills not generally called on in mainstream curriculum. Ashley and Kayleigh faced personal challenges, but took responsibility and met them. They now know that they have something valuable they can offer.

'Oh, you're naughty! Oh, you're cool!'

The research was conducted in an 11–18 mixed comprehensive of 1050 students serving a wide area of South London and parts of West London. Some areas it recruits from are prosperous, while others are marked by poverty and dislocation; the school's intake reflects these polarities.

Teachers in the Design and Technology (D&T) department were asked to suggest any students who were competent but who were diffident or disruptive. Three Year 8 students were identified (two boys, Kurt and Graham, and one girl, Lauren) who were known to be talented but whose talents were not always obvious in lessons. The idea was to give these students the opportunity to teach younger students, drawing on their own interests and expertise, and to see if this would have a positive effect on their self-esteem, motivation or image.

The three student teachers were interviewed individually for about 30 minutes, once before the teaching episode with Year 7s and once after. During the earlier interviews, they were asked about their interests in D&T, both inside and outside school, and about things they enjoyed in school and things they didn't like or would like to change. The later interviews attempted to gain an insight into how the student teachers evaluated the lessons they had taught. Group interviews were conducted with the Y7 students. Interviews were recorded and transcribed. D&T teachers were asked to make a note of any observed changes in behaviour or attitude of the student teachers during the project, however trivial.

Seven weeks after the teaching episodes, short questionnaires were circulated to all teachers who were in regular contact with the student teachers. They were asked for evidence of any changes in the students' motivation, self-esteem and attitude to learning. 50% (26/52) of the questionnaires were returned. The interview data were contextualised by analysing the students' interim school reports, both before and after the teaching episodes, and through teachers' informal conversations and written comments. The researcher also recorded his observations of the lessons taught.

The three student teachers

Lauren is 13 years old and in Year 8. She joined the school in Year 7 with above-average grades from primary school. However, she has increasingly become argumentative and confrontational with her teachers and at times with her peers and has low self-esteem. She has often been in trouble and her negative attitude to school and learning caused concern in all subjects; her mother has been invited to the school to discuss her progress on numerous occasions. Lauren recently came off her green report card, which she had been on for nearly a year. She explained that there was a certain kudos associated with being on report:

> When you're on it you're kind of proud of it because everyone goes, 'Oh, you're naughty! Oh, you're cool! You're on target cards' and you think you're really clever.

Lauren's attainment grades have steadily declined in all subjects and there is evidence that she only does homework in two subjects. She is in detention almost daily. Her most recent school report showed no improvement. Lauren acknowledges that she is 'chatty and sometimes disrespectful … quite naughty and always has an answer'. She believes that this is because she gets bored and is then easily distracted. She also feels incredibly frustrated in many of her classes as she feels she has things she wants to say but is never given the opportunity to do so:

> Sometimes you're in lessons and you have an opinion on what they're saying but you can't say it because you'd get into trouble or it's not your turn to speak.

> The problem with me is if a teacher shouts at me I don't shut up and listen, I argue back …

She feels that her Y7 reputation has preceded her and that some teachers refuse to forget this:

> I think I earned myself a bad reputation in Year 7 and now they don't like me that much, which is not very good for me. They don't believe me when I say I am trying to be good. They say, 'You don't know how to be good.' I think if you come into this school you have to be good from the beginning and then you earn the respect from the teachers.

Lauren recognises that her relationships with most of her teachers – including her form tutor – are not good and she feels that she is partly to blame for this:

> It's not Miss X's fault [her form tutor]. It's just that I see her at the end of the day for registration and by that time I've had enough.

Kurt is 12 years old and in Year 8. He found the transition from primary to secondary school difficult and his attendance has been sporadic. At one time the problem was so acute that Kurt was on the verge of becoming a school phobic. He was anxious about missing schoolwork because of his sometimes lengthy periods of non-attendance and this anxiety made him reluctant to come to school. His attainment levels are not a true reflection of his capability. He might be perceived as introverted and lacking in self-confidence, but he is in fact articulate and thoughtful; he takes time to think before he speaks and is quietly spoken almost to the point where he can be inaudible at times. His teachers recognise that he has to be dealt with sensitively. He was pleased to be chosen for the project but expressed reservations to his form tutor as he did not want to miss lessons as a result of taking part in the project (he was given reassurance about this).

Graham is 12 years old and also in Year 8. He is highly motivated, attains high levels in most of his subjects and always completes his homework tasks. He admits to being 'loud and bossy' and says that he 'likes to put his opinions across'. He has positive relationships with his teachers and his form tutor reported recently that Graham is 'very polite and conscientious'. He has a small circle of close friends but has been the subject of verbal bullying from others because of his positive attitude towards learning; in some classes, they shout out while he attempts to answer questions. As a result, Graham is losing confidence and has become withdrawn. In Art and Design lessons, however, he is lively and continues to do good work.

Thus, we have three very different student teachers: Lauren, who is straightforwardly disaffected and difficult, and Kurt and Graham who are not noisily disruptive but who can lack confidence, are anxious in school and are in danger of becoming disengaged.

What students enjoy in and out of school

All three students were invited to take part in the project because they showed potential in D&T. During the interviews they all said that they liked practical things – like acting Romeo and Juliet in English, 'instead of always reading and writing' (Lauren) or 'making a newspaper in History using desktop publishing software' (Kurt).

Kurt commented:

> There are no subjects that I like but there are some things I actually like. I actually enjoy doing Design ... It's quite lively and I actually like challenges.

He went on:

> I like using computers and things like that but what I actually really do like in school is when they give you a choice of multiple choices of what you can do and then loads of people come up with these really good designs and you learn things.

Students were also asked what their interests were outside the formal curriculum and in particular outside school. Lauren's Mum had taught her how to cook and she does a lot of cooking at home. She enjoys Food Technology and often helps her peers in class; she says she finds it 'easy to explain' things to them. Lauren has a more positive relationship with her Food Technology teacher and because of this and her expertise in cooking outside school she was invited to join the project; she taught a small group of Y7 students.

Kurt and Graham are friends and had worked on a Formula 1 (F1) Car Project together. This was a national competition undertaken as an extra-curricular activity within the D&T department. Their relationship developed whilst working collaboratively on this project and after winning several regional finals, they won the National Final for Key Stage 3. The success of the Formula 1 work had done much for Kurt's confidence, self-esteem and attendance. It was thought that participation in the present project might help sustain this confidence. Because they had such a good relationship, it was thought that Kurt and Graham could work together but plan and teach distinct parts of the same lesson.

The student teachers' views of school

In the preliminary interviews all three spoke about wanting to be able to make their own decisions about the things they did in class. Both Graham and Kurt also said they wanted to be challenged as opposed to being given 'easy work'.

Graham spoke passionately about the distinction between the nature of the work he undertook for the F1 Project and what happens in some of his other lessons:

> [In the F1 project] we were given time limits and we were just given an outline of what to do, whereas normally we get told how to do it and everything ... I didn't actually know about aerodynamics so I actually had to do the research and think about what I was doing and we could actually make it a bit different.

Graham went on:

> You always get set work. You have to do this, you have to do that. It's not like a multiple choice. Like in History this week we had a choice of what topic we wanted to do, like transportation and culture, so you had a choice and that was good so we didn't end up doing some silly topic that you don't like.

During the F1 Project Kurt liked seeing whether his ideas would work or not:

> I like the tension of the things that happen and go wrong and waiting and watching.

Kurt described how good he felt when he made things:

> When you actually make it I always find myself feeling quite pleased.

Kurt also likes art, drawing and modelling his ideas using computers. Kurt summed up his school experience in the following comment:

> I think teachers should expect more of us. If they actually do give us a bit more opportunity to actually think for ourselves and stuff then we might do it. I think things can still be hard and challenging but they can also still be quite fun.

Such insights are not uncommon and echo some of the findings from the research undertaken by Shultz and Cook-Sather (2001):

> … we are continually amazed and inspired by how much students think about their own education and how their attention demands ours … we learned again that students think deeply about educational issues, they have striking insights into them, and they have a great deal to say about them.

The teaching episodes

Lessons at the school are 35 minutes long. The D&T department operates a carousel system throughout Key Stage 3 whereby students experience a number of different projects designed to develop skills, knowledge and understanding in areas such as graphics, systems and control and materials technology. Food Technology has been introduced this year as part of the carousel. The students who were to be involved in each of the teaching episodes were selected to reflect the diverse nature of the Y7 school population. It was important for the study not to set up teaching episodes with student groups who were all high ability and very well-behaved. Each teaching group comprised two male and two female students. Barry and Charlie (in Lauren's group) were described by their teachers as 'very challenging, having poor concentration and often in trouble'.

The student teachers decided on the subject matter for their respective lessons. They knew that they could, if they wanted to, ask for help from their D&T teachers when planning their lessons. Lauren took up the offer of help and liaised on several occasions with her food teacher but she had her own ideas and planned the lesson herself; it included an end-of-lesson evaluation. Kurt and Graham chose to be independent and planned their lesson on their own.

All the student teachers thought teaching a lesson would be a new experience and a real challenge but they also confessed to being nervous. All were worried about the students' behaviour. When they found out who the students were, Graham and Kurt wanted to know if they could change one or two who they thought had the potential to misbehave.

Lauren was particularly worried about whether the students would listen and follow instructions:

> If they don't respect us because we're only children ... I know children are rude because I backchat my teachers when they annoy me so if I shout at them and they shout back I'll be a bit ... I won't know what to do.

She was understandably nervous just before the lesson and said, 'I'm going to be good to my teachers from now on.'

Lauren's lesson

Lauren taught a triple food lesson which spanned both morning and lunchtime breaks, finishing before afternoon break. The room was meticulously organised. She had her lesson plan in front of her, the worksheets were photocopied, a food demonstration area had been designated and the ingredients arranged in sequential order, down to the last grain! Lauren looked the part. She seemed far smarter than I had been used to in our earlier encounters. She decided to put her blazer on prior to the lesson. It was clear to me that she not only had put a lot of work into the planning and preparation for this lesson, but she seemed to be relishing the role of playing teacher. Her whole demeanour suggested that she had a sense of purpose, a responsibility and that she was up for it!

Lauren introduced the learning objectives and using the board proceeded to list the aims for the lesson. She was confident and showed no signs of her earlier nerves. The first part of the lesson covered basic food hygiene. She involved the students by asking lots of open-ended questions: for example, 'Why is it important to wash your hands in Food Technology?' If students were struggling to provide answers Lauren did not answer her own questions but re-worded them or gave clues, ensuring that the students were thinking for themselves. She showed a high degree of skill in questioning students.

Lauren then demonstrated the skills and knowledge needed for the students to make fairy cakes. The demonstration was thoroughly planned and delivered. The sequencing of the tasks was highlighted and clearly explained and the pace was right. Lauren used appropriate technical vocabulary at all times, citing correctly the names of the equipment and ingredients. Her use of language was simple but effective. She emphasised key points and offered tips such as, 'Mind your egg doesn't roll off the table.' She also showed a sense of humour: 'It happened to me once but I blamed my wonky kitchen table'. The students listened attentively, making notes, as requested, for later reference. It was, in many ways, a model demonstration.

After lunch (lesson 2), the students began making their cakes. Lauren moved round the group, seeing students in turn and at regular intervals. She gave help, offered advice and gave further instructions when necessary. One of the boys didn't know how to use the weighing scales so Lauren explained this again, slowly covering all the necessary information. When the students were getting on, Lauren would show foresight and prepare the resources needed for the next stage. Lauren also had health and safety in mind, reminding students that the oven doors get very hot and of the hazards of leaving them open.

On one occasion, towards the end of the lesson, the boys started to offer silly answers to the evaluation questions and to giggle. Lauren, without raising her voice, and in a calm but assertive manner, told the boys to 'stop being silly'; she added, 'Let's take this seriously or it will not work'. The boys did and the lesson continued to flow. The atmosphere throughout was calm, productive, positive, safe and humorous. There seemed to be a real sense of community. Even when tidying away and washing up – usually a real bone of contention in Food Technology – everyone helped.

Graham and Kurt's lesson

Graham and Kurt decided to teach a double lesson that had two distinct but related learning aims. Kurt would teach the first part – how to sketch two-dimensional (2D) ideas using pencils and paper. Graham would teach the second part which was to use the sketches to produce a three-dimensional (3D) computer aided design (CAD) of their pencil sketches. This was the most ambitious of all the teaching episodes. Many students find sketching and generating ideas difficult and the 3D CAD package that they were going to use is one that both trainee trainees and experienced teachers have found difficult to master.

Both Graham and Kurt were in the classroom making final preparations just before the start of the lesson. Some of the students walked in without being invited and Graham asked, 'Are you here for the teaching project?' One of the Year 7 girls answered enthusiastically. Graham responded: 'Can you just wait outside until we ask you to come in?' He seemed to be taking on the persona of a teacher from the beginning. Graham then drew a two-dimensional (2D) and a three-dimensional (3D) sketch on the board. Kurt was sketching a picture of a trout, his visual aid to help him explain aerodynamics. A simplified definition of aerodynamics is the study of forces acting on a mass (or object) through things such as air and water. It is one of the concepts necessary to understand when designing the shapes of racing cars which need to be able to pass through air with the minimum of force in order to record the fastest racing time.

Kurt and Graham gave a joint presentation, giving a brief outline of the focus and scope of the lesson. This was clear and covered the learning aims for both sections. Kurt then demonstrated how to make a sketch using pencils and paper. He also showed the parts of a design he had done based on the aerodynamic shape of a trout, pointing out the thin profile and smooth surface of the trout. He explained that this aerodynamic shape made it easier for the trout to swim through the water. This demonstration was satisfactory although he seemed nervous and perhaps rushed things a little. He went on to explain that their designs had to fit inside a rectangular shape, which represented the length and width of the machine's manufacturing capacity. Kurt explained this by drawing a rectangular box and specified the sizes by using a ruler and pencil. The students were then asked to design their ideas by first drawing their rectangular boxes.

As the students settled down it became quite clear that at least two of them were confused about the relationship between the rectangular box, the aerodynamic trout and the generation of their own ideas. Kurt responded by explaining one to one. Graham supported his friend. When helping one to one, at no time did Kurt attempt to take control of the pencil and do the work for the students. Instead, he would say, 'I won't actually draw it for you'. He was very conscious of their personal space and made sure that he gave all students the attention they needed. He used praise saying, 'I really like your design,' and, 'That's a good idea. It's even better than my first ideas when I did this project.' By the end of the first section of the lesson, the students each had a sketch of an idea ready to put onto the computer.

Graham then organised the students around one of the computer monitors and introduced the CAD program. He used a form of scaffolding, carefully progressing from a 2D rectangle drawing on the board and covered in Kurt's lesson to a 3D rectangle drawing also on the board, to a 3D CAD rectangular form. This was the starting point for students to draw their own CAD designs. Graham had also produced a step-by-step booklet for each of the students but failed to refer to it. Throughout his demonstration, Graham spoke with confidence, but he rushed things. His technical knowledge and use of appropriate language were excellent, however.

As the students logged on to the computers and began to use the CAD program, it quickly transpired that they were confused. There were two reasons for this. The first was the nature of the CAD program with its complex interface and array of CAD tools and drop down menus – and the idea of designing using computers was a completely new experience for these Y7 students. Second, some of the students had already had difficulty understanding the concepts of length and width when drawing the rectangle with Kurt, and now Graham had introduced another variable – breadth.

It is not unusual for students to experience difficulties with these concepts. The way Graham and Kurt responded was interesting. At first, Graham tried to address the students' problems as Kurt had done, on a one-to-one basis. He even said, 'I probably didn't explain it that well, so I will show you individually.' He did not blame the students for not listening; nor did he think that the task was too difficult for them. After a few minutes he seemed to sense that all the students had a common misunderstanding and that he needed to adopt a different strategy so he asked the group to gather round the computer again and he gave another demonstration. This time, however, the pace was noticeably slower, his explanations clearer and he decided to reduce the amount of information, breaking it down into bitesize bits. Graham involved the group by asking questions; he was probing their understanding: 'What measurement do you want?' and 'Why do you need to...?' This time he made better use of the booklet he had designed. Each time the students would go back and draw their ideas, using the CAD program. Graham would help them, offer advice, make sure they were all right and reassure them. He used appropriate technical language and was aware of time, giving students regular targets against the clock.

The lesson was in many ways astonishing: within 90 minutes, students had come up with a pencil design and a 3D CAD model of their ideas; they were using the CAD package, albeit at a basic level, and this was a real achievement.

Whilst Graham had been teaching, Kurt had been busy doing something on the computer. It was only when he asked the group to gather round towards the end of Graham's part of the lesson that it became clear what he had been doing. He explained again the aerodynamic shape of the trout. This time, however, he had attempted to improve his demonstration by supplementing his original pencil sketches of the trout with a CAD drawing of a trout he had been working on whilst Graham had been teaching. The students could now see the whole process, the transformation between aerodynamic trout pencil sketch to trout-inspired CAD drawing, and it made sense to them.

This episode gave several insights into Kurt's thinking. It showed that he was able to reflect critically on the reasons why his approach had not been effective; he knew that an alternative framework was required. It also showed that he had both the confidence and perseverance to continue, despite the earlier setback of knowing that his original demonstration had not been good. Given Kurt's anxious nature, this was evidence of real commitment and self-discipline.

The student teachers' reflections

All three student teachers spoke positively about the experience and said that they would like the opportunity to teach again. When asked what they thought they had learned from the experience, they commented on different things.

Lauren reflected on her relationships with her teachers. She could see the student–teacher interaction from both the teacher's and the students' perspective and she had learned:

> Not to be horrible to teachers because ... it's intimidating for them to get up in front of a group of people, especially if there's only one of you and there's more of them.

She was surprised at just how much planning and preparation was required to teach a lesson. '[I had to] think up some questions about basic health and safety and do a worksheet', and 'the [planning] took me ages.' Lauren recalls the time when one of her teachers remonstrated with her: 'She said, "I have spent two hours preparing this lesson", and I said, "I never asked you to prepare it."' She realised now what a lot of planning is involved and with hindsight she felt sorry about making those comments to her teacher. She described standing up in front of the class as frightening, with four pairs of eyes watching your every move and four pairs of ears listening to your every word. Lauren spoke about her use of language: she had made a conscious effort to say things clearly, using words that students would understand but in 'proper English'. She recalled her own feelings when teachers spoke to her as if she were a child and she had tried to avoid doing this to her group:

> I know how annoying it is if the teacher stands and talks to you like you're five years old because they think you don't understand ... I just tried to talk to them at a level that they normally talk to their friends at, I suppose.

She was self-critical, pointing out that the beginning of the lesson, when she was nervous, 'could have been better' but she knew that the demonstration had gone well. Reflecting on the whole experience, she was enormously proud of what she had achieved.

She said it was a lot of hard work but it paid off because the students said they enjoyed it and it was fun:

> *Makes me feel, I don't know, proud in a way that I have done it and they [the students] really enjoyed it.*

Kurt thought his teaching episode 'wasn't exactly brilliant' but added, 'Well, I think I didn't explain it that well in the beginning and I thought I needed to do it again'. He thought that his second explanation was far better. The best part of the lesson for Kurt was when the students 'grasped how to do natural designs'. Graham admitted that he thought that the students would not listen and therefore not learn anything. This made him rush his introduction on how to use the CAD program and he forgot about the booklets he had prepared. He was happier with his step-by-step approach and thought that from then on the lesson 'went to plan really' although the CAD package 'was a little confusing for them'. Nevertheless:

> *I think they did learn something, which was good because I thought they were not going to listen or learn anything but they actually managed to ... They did actually learn the basics and I think that was the objective really. So I was pleased with that.*

He went on:

> *It was nice to have some power 'cos you don't normally have that in a lesson or at school. So it was nice to tell people what to do instead of getting told what to do.*

All three student teachers recognised that they were only teaching four students and Lauren said, 'Imagine what it would be like with 30 of them.'

What the Year 7s thought of the student teachers

The Y7 students, who were interviewed immediately after the two lessons, all spoke positively about the 'lesson' and they commented on a number of points. Steve thought that although being taught by a Y8 student was strange at first, there wasn't 'much of a difference', from being taught by his usual teachers. Barry, in the other group, expressed the same opinion. Many of the students mentioned how easy it was to understand the student teachers. Denise said it was like 'talking to a friend', and Will said you could speak how you wanted to them and they would understand.

Lisa commented:

> It was interesting, like their vocabulary and how they kind of said it. Because if a teacher had have said it to you they'd have used more, like different language. It was like talking to somebody your own age; they said it quite clearly so you could understand them.

Lauren's group thought that she explained things very well both to the whole group during demonstrations and on a one-to-one basis, 'So it was like, it was really good the way she did it' (Denise). Lisa, from Kurt and Graham's group, admitted that measurement was, 'not one of my talents,' but said that her student teacher explained it clearly and 'encouraged you' – and added that Graham's booklet was 'really helpful and useful'.

The Y7s thought the student teachers were like 'real teachers' but they noticed some moments when things went a bit wrong:

> When she was demonstrating it she did it slow and well. But when she was doing it like she kind of messed up a few bits, but that was understandable. But she did it like so that you could understand ... If she was to be a teacher she would be a good teacher. **–Denise**

Will agreed:

> I thought she taught well because she done all the things that a teacher would normally do. And as she was like writing everything on the board she would write it a lot slower so you could understand it and everything. And she come round to everyone and helped them if they needed help.

Y7s from the other group were also impressed by their student teachers:

> It's really fun and that, being taught by them. They just put enjoyment into it. I wasn't gonna come in today, but I'm glad I did. **–Charlie**

However, the Y7s had one reservation about the idea of student teachers. It focused on status and being told what to do by people just a little older than themselves. Charlie saw the funny side of this but Barry admitted to feeling awkward when being told off.

> It was all right [laughs]. It was a bit weird, like I was getting, like they were being a bit bossy [laughs]. I don't have a problem with it. **–Charlie**

> Well being told off was a bit annoying because like, it's like just being told by someone that doesn't really have the rights to tell you. **–Barry**

I asked about the incident when Lauren told Will and Steve to 'stop mucking about':

> I thought that it felt kind of embarrassing, because getting told off by a Year 8, then as we got, like, right to the end I realised why she was doing it. So that we could get through the lesson more quick. **–Will**

Barry questioned whether all students would listen to student teachers:

> When a teacher's teaching you, some kids are naughty for teachers. But if they're naughty for a teacher, what would it be like if they had another student teaching them? They're not exactly just going to sit in their seats and do what they're told. They're going to be all over the place messing things up. **–Barry**

During Lauren's teaching episode, Will had said to Lauren: 'I thought you were naughty.' I asked him why he had said this. He replied:

> Oh yeah, because normally she's always getting detention and she'll be naughty a lot. That's what she said before we started. But the way she was acting there, it was sort of like she was a good student.

I asked the Y7 students if they would like the opportunity to be student teachers. Out of the eight students who took part, seven of them said yes and the other one didn't know. Lisa said she might if she could do one of her favourite subjects but that she would have to practise the lesson a couple of times so that she was clear about what she was doing. Even Barry, despite his earlier reservations, said 'Yeah, I would personally, it would be quite fun. I thought they thought it was fun.' Lisa explained how valuable it was to see the classroom from a different perspective:

> ... it gives you the chance to see how [your teacher feels] when she teaches loads of children ... Like, say you're really naughty and you've got children to do it, it would give you the chance to see how they feel when they've been like, when they've had a hard day's work like with screaming kids and like with having to shout all day and go over all the work a couple of times. -Lisa

What was the impact on the student teachers?

Lauren was particularly pleased at being chosen to participate in the project and, even before the teaching episodes took place, there seemed to be a change in her overall attitude and in her relationship with her teachers. She gave a 'Thank-you' card to her form tutor, showing a side to her that was rarely, if ever, seen. During one of her Food Technology lessons, shortly before her teaching episode, she took offence at being asked to be quiet and stormed out of the lesson theatrically (not unusual) declaring that she didn't want to take part in the project. Two days later she sheepishly approached her Food teacher, apologising and asking if she could still be involved in the project. On another occasion she said to her Food teacher:

> Thanks, Miss, for giving me this opportunity. Other teachers would not have given me this opportunity because of my reputation.

These were unusual behaviours for Lauren. This positive attitude continued for the rest of the term. She went to see her Food teacher the day after the teaching episode under the pretence of looking for her Food book – and she asked how she had done. Her Food teacher told her that she had taught a brilliant lesson and, for the first time, Lauren's face went visibly red. She was also seen outside the head of year's room again, but this time she was handing in homework and not waiting to be given a detention. The deputy headteacher said: 'We must build on the positive effect this project has had on Lauren.'

Later, during the school's festivities week, Lauren was asked to help in a 'Ready Steady Cook' type presentation. This involved assisting the visiting chefs in preparing a recipe in front of the whole school. Her Food Technology teacher said that she rose to the occasion, enjoyed being in the limelight and knew exactly what to do when helping. Her teachers described her as being more confident and mature and less argumentative. Her form tutor said that she had developed a better relationship with Lauren and that Lauren now realised that teachers were there to help:

> Totally different student to the first term. She is friendly and cooperative nearly all the time. **–Subject teacher**

> Better relationship with myself. Not so quick to fly off the handle. More cooperative, polite and says 'hello' now! **–Form tutor**

Many of Graham's teachers noticed an improvement in his motivation and self-esteem. He had the confidence to take part in discussions and was more assertive when his peers interrupted him:

> He is more relaxed and comfortable with himself. He takes part in class discussions and even when an overloud student tries to talk him down he will stick up for himself. **–Form tutor**

> He is much more confident and I have noticed improvement in self-esteem. He is answering questions and participating in debates more frequently. **–Subject teacher**

Kurt also benefited:

He has developed more confidence and is much more motivated to learn and take part in school activities. –**Form tutor**

It would seem that, in the short term at least, the three students had all 'developed' in their own ways. All were able to rise to the challenge of teaching their 'specialist' skills to a group of younger peers. In doing so, they demonstrated that they could be both responsible and motivated. Above all, they seemed to show a high level of maturity when reflecting on their experience. They were aware of the necessity of planning, could look at student behaviour from the teacher's perspective and recognise what made classroom strategies effective. In this respect, all students gained an invaluable insight into the world of a teacher and spoke candidly about it.

Kurt's early signs of self-confidence were sustained and Graham's self-confidence returned and he began to participate in classroom discussions once again. Lauren seemed to develop most, though. From being a student with negative attitudes towards her teachers and her schoolwork, she gained in self-respect and showed greater respect for her teachers. She was doing homework again and had not only been asked by the school to participate in a high-profile event – the demonstration with the visiting chefs – but rose to the occasion. Perhaps, even more importantly, being a student teacher had allowed Lauren to show a more sensitive, warmer side – which seemed to have been smothered by the endless stream of report cards and detentions.

Sustaining it

During the next academic year I went back to the school to interview, separately, all three students. I also analysed school reports and sent questionnaires, via the student teachers, to their respective teachers. Both Graham and Kurt managed to get their teachers to return 71% of the questionnaires, whereas Lauren 'selected' 50% of her teachers to complete them. Graham and Kurt had continued to make excellent progress. Kurt's attendance and overall attainment had improved in most subjects. Kurt's History teacher, who had taught him last year, reported that he contributed well in class and was more confident. His Maths teacher reported that he had 'grown in confidence this year'. Kurt's relationship with Graham continued to thrive and Graham was, according to several teachers, participating well in class.

Lauren, however, had missed many weeks of schooling as a result of two 'enormous' fights at the beginning of the new school year, one involving students within the school and one involving ten students from another school. Her relationship with her teachers seemed still to be positive, but this may have been a reflection of her careful selection of respondents when she handed out the questionnaires to her teachers. They wrote that Lauren was, 'a pleasure to teach', that they 'enjoyed teaching Lauren' and that she was 'utterly charming most of the time'. Despite the short-term gains in the period following the teaching episode, Lauren had slipped back a bit in some areas of her work and behaviour; she may have needed more sustained support and patient encouragement.

'I love art but I can't stand school'

This chapter focuses on Mark and Jason, two artistically inclined but otherwise disengaged students attending a large state comprehensive school. Mark and Jason were in Year 9 at the beginning of the study in 2003; Jason was suspended from school during the initial period, but the study follows his progress into Year 10. I worked with two teachers, Sharon, the head of the Art and Design department, and Diane, at that time a trainee teacher of Art and Design.

The school is a welcoming and highly regarded institution. Its students appear by and large to be happy and motivated but with the usual complaints about lessons and school regulations. It was suggested to me by a Year 10 student, for example, that the school could be improved by 'getting rid of lunchtime detention, especially for things like untidy uniform'. The school is seen, in terms of examination results and other measures of performance, as high achieving. In particular, the Art and Design department has been very successful in attaining well-above-average examination results. The Art and Design department, and the school as a whole, are efficiently run and effective in terms of their stated goals.

Although not badly behaved when compared with students in some other schools, Mark and Jason stood out in this school as being rather difficult. They were selected because they showed promise in their performance in Art and Design lessons while being disaffected with other aspects of school life. The overall aim of the study was to explore the potential of an approach that focuses on and develops the positive leadership qualities of students who are currently seen by their teachers and peers as modelling anti-schoolwork attitudes and behaviours.

Young people increasingly find opportunities for self-expression and exploration of personal identities out of the classroom. The lack of opportunity for self-expression in school can lead to disengagement from the school's learning purposes. Art and Design is one subject area that can offer many opportunities to re-establish this engagement. It can encourage self-expression and address issues of personal identity. However, as with the rest of the curriculum, the pressures associated with raising the school's profile through academic achievement and test results can often squeeze out such concerns.

There was a perceived need within the school to promote a stronger sense of the institution as an inclusive learning community. We wanted to find out whether focusing on the development of positive leadership qualities in Art would help disengaged students to build self-esteem and self-motivation and change the way that others habitually saw them.

In identifying students who might benefit from participating in this study, three criteria were used:

- first, we found out whether they had 'unschooled' art skills, and had an active interest in producing artwork outside of school
- second, whether they demonstrated negative leadership among their peers
- third, how they behaved in other classes, outside Art.

Mark

Mark, from Year 9, was the first to be identified. In Year 8 he had been designated by the school as 'gifted and talented' – a term that he often uses in talking about himself – but had become disengaged during Year 9, achieving only average attainment and effort grades in Art. However, he continued to develop a high level of detailed observational drawings outside school, keeping them in a sketchbook. Within school, although potentially a high achieving student, he would often become involved in off-task behaviour and was at times the catalyst for disruptive behaviour in the class. Within Art lessons he occasionally appeared to take his status as a 'gifted and talented' student for granted, and was easily distracted; at times, he showed negative leadership qualities in Art, particularly amongst his male peers.

The preliminary research included observations of Mark throughout a school day in other curriculum areas, as well as informal discussions with him about the nature of his out-of-school art-making. He explained that, 'Mum and Dad and other people in the class say that my sketchbooks are good, but I don't think I am the top star of the class.' He often visited galleries – especially on family visits to Toronto. Asked what kind of art he liked he responded, 'I don't like Cubism, but I like real life sketching of things like cars and have drawn a rugby pitch.' He thought that he might like to be an architect when he left school.

Planning the teaching episode

His Art teachers talked to him and introduced the notion of teaching other students. The conversation was recorded and gave some important insights into how Mark perceived himself in school and his thoughts about the teaching task. Mark is straightforward in talking about himself and his feelings and he told his teachers, 'When you first mentioned it I was scared, but now it has been explained, I think I will find it easy.' One thing worried him – the possibility of spontaneity: 'I won't find it hard, but I think I will find it challenging if I have to make it up on the spot.' His teachers knew that he would need help with the planning in order to feel secure.

He explained that he was keen to take on the art teaching role because in his Art lessons he had become frustrated with the progress of others in his class, particularly in a recent lesson which involved experimenting with various marks:

> I was talking to them when we were doing the clay fish and some of them said that they just wanted to get on with making the fish and didn't want to do the mark-making because they thought it would ruin it.

And so Mark decided to do a 'mark-making' exercise himself. ('Mark-making' is a general term used among Art teachers to refer to activities in Art lessons which focus on students using a variety of media, such as rollers, brushes, pencils – in fact, anything which can make a mark – in order to develop students' range of expressive skills and extend their visual repertoire.) This type of lesson is commonplace in schools and reflects a particular kind of orthodoxy with which Mark was clearly familiar.

When asked how he felt about teaching this session to his peers, he said:

> Other people are always asking me for help during the lesson because I am 'gifted and talented'. I find it pretty easy telling everyone else what to do.

But he was also concerned about taking on a more formal teaching role: 'I am worried that they will not listen to me as I am the same age as them' (the teaching episode was to involve other students in the same year group rather than younger students). He was also asked whether he thought that taking on a teaching role would change his relationship with the class; he replied:

> I think it will change, especially with my friends; they will look up to me more and ask me what to do more. I won't mind telling them what to do.

Two meetings were arranged between Mark and his Art and Design teachers with the intention of planning the lesson, including the preparation of any resources. Mark decided that it would be useful to make exemplary material:

'If the kids can see how I have done it, it will be easier for them to understand.' He displayed a high level of understanding about teaching strategies that would be effective. He suggested ideas and spoke about lessons he had experienced which he felt had worked. He also talked persuasively about the characteristics of a good teacher:

> You use your hands a lot to show, you show the children how to do it first. Then the children can look at it and think – wow that's brilliant, I could do that! You also show different techniques and you break up information that you give and then they can do it. Don't take it the wrong way, but I sometimes like to do it my own way.

In preparation, Mark created a worksheet for the students to use to practise mark-making techniques, concentrating on form, contour and plane.

Mark also demonstrated insight in planning the lesson, and a capacity to analyse the nature of teaching and learning in a constructive way:

> I think it is easier to look at something and draw it rather than making it up in your head, but then when you do draw something from your head you are proud of it because it is yours.

His choice of subject, although not the most engaging, had a rationale that reflected his observation that his peers do not take much notice of mark-making and often rush to complete their artwork without considering the range of visual techniques at their disposal. Mark also decided to structure the activities in steps, to use his own artwork as a resource, and to demonstrate each activity himself:

> I want to do it step by step and on a big scale. ... I want to demonstrate on the big scale drawing on the table so that the children can see, using block colour and tonal work. ... They've got to understand how to use tone and light. [...] I have the idea that they should practise mark-making of a sphere first as there are a lot of rounded shapes in the montage. This will help to blend in the idea of mark-making and the picture.

Mark was clearly planning according to how he felt a teacher would teach the lesson. It is interesting that he chose to refer to his peers as 'the children', reinforcing perhaps the 'us and them' structures of regular classroom relationships.

Mark's teaching episode

Mark's lesson took place in the usual teaching room, at the normal lesson time, with the rest of his class. It became clear during the lesson that the original intention of allowing Mark full responsibility for the lesson could not be realised. Although he was able to lead part of the lesson, more direction of students and class management were considered by Sharon to be required. At the start of the lesson, his peers displayed a cynical attitude towards both the situation and Mark. They audibly directed questions to the teachers who were present such as:

> Is Mark going to be the teacher today, Miss?
>
> We don't get it, Miss. He's rubbish. Can you explain it?

During this initial phase, Mark's nervousness was apparent and the students in the class were amused and unsettled. Some became restless, saying they did not understand what he required them to do. However, Mark remained calm, although uncomfortable. It was at this stage that Sharon and Diane took more of a classroom management role. It is likely that the very presence of the class's usual teachers affected the dynamics of the lesson and took away Mark's authority. Once the students were on task, Mark visibly relaxed and chose to walk around the class and help with any queries. At this stage, the students responded well to him, some asking for advice and others eager to receive his attention. Mark then demonstrated transferring the learning about mark-making to the composition.

At this point, he shifted from taking a leading role to being on the same level as his peers. He re-established his position as one of the students, and played no further part as leader. Instead, he concentrated on finishing the larger scale piece with another student, and spent very little time observing or looking at the work of other students. His manner also shifted from being serious to becoming more disruptive and clownish, possibly to reinforce his position within the group and to indicate to his peers that he was still one of them.

Most students successfully completed the worksheet and started to transfer their understanding to their composition, demonstrating that learning was taking place. Following the lesson many students were interested to know how we felt Mark had performed, and two girls commented that being a teacher must be quite hard if you have to stand up in front of a class like them.

Mark was encouraged to reflect upon the lesson in a follow-up interview conducted by Diane.

He was asked how he felt about the lesson generally and he confessed to feeling very uneasy at first:

> I was very nervous at the start of the lesson, especially because people kept asking me questions but the questions helped me a lot because I could deal with their questions pretty easily ...

He also thought on reflection that he should have experimented more beforehand – and used a different pen:

> When I was doing the big picture at the front table [the large-scale demonstration] I think the pen was too thick for doing the contouring but it worked on the stippling and the controlled scribbling. ... If I had done it with the thin pen beforehand ... It did work though and Adam helped me do it – he liked doing that!

When asked about the impact of the lesson, he said he thought that the students had learned a lot more about aspects of mark-making and that they found the session useful:

> They learnt much more about the type of work, all about the dimensions like flat, plane, shape, contour and form and when I was in the picnic area [during break after the lesson] they said it was good how I had shown them different ways of using tone around plane and form.

Moreover, he was pleased that the class settled down and became attentive: 'I don't think anyone talked when I was teaching, so that was good, yeah, it was a good lesson.'

He also mentioned that the class 'look up to me now … they appreciate me'. Asked about whether he felt that his relationship with his peers had really changed he confirmed that it had – for the better, adding again that 'they look up to me more … It went well'. He expanded on this point in ways that indicate the complexities of peer relationships:

> They [looked up to me before] because they knew I was gifted and talented, but now they appreciate me. They appreciated me showing them how to use tone and dimension. ... I think it helped me in the class because they look up to me now and they saw me take a lesson.

Overall, it was a positive experience for Mark and he seemed keen to try a similar activity again.

The two Art and Design teachers reflected on this first phase of the project in order to inform any subsequent activity. There were some aspects of the peer-teaching event which needed addressing; in particular, it was clear that the traditional roles of teacher and student were reinforced by having the teachers present. Mark himself commented on the difficulties of managing 'his' lesson when teachers were actively present:

> I think if I did the lesson on my own, it would have been a lot different if you didn't help me.

At the same time, he said that he valued the teachers' guidance and support:

> I hadn't done anything like that before, and it was all new to me, so you helped me. That helped me a lot.

However, the situation was complicated by the fact that the lesson took place under the usual school conditions, including lesson duration – complete with bells – and the fact that the teaching episode took place in the same location as a normal Art lesson. The two teachers involved felt that more attention needed to be given to the choice of a topic. Mark had planned the lesson with them but without consulting other students, although he had some ideas for alternative topics that might have engaged them more – and the planning sessions were confined to only two meetings. Mark chose a topic which he felt a teacher would choose (and one which the group had already been less than enthusiastic about); he was not in fact confident enough to try out his own ideas for topics. It was not surprising therefore that the group was neither excited nor engaged by the mark-making topic: it was a 'schoolish' kind of lesson without the benefit of being delivered by a school professional.

The teachers and the researcher concluded that it would be desirable in any replication of the project to:

- allow further time for planning the activity
- allow more time for the preparation of the materials
- in the planning, consult other students in addition to teachers
- allow a more natural input from the student teachers, so that they can teach what they think their peers would enjoy.

Mark had mentioned in the first meeting that he felt that some of the boys would like to draw cars:

> It's good to do a project that we would really like to do. I don't know about the girls, but boys would like to do cars and do what they like on them.

He could have been encouraged to pursue this possibility (albeit in a more inclusive way) but with a smaller group of students who had expressed interest in the chosen topic. Taking the teaching outside the usual structures of the classroom and time slot might also have heightened engagement and the meaningfulness of the activity and created a less cynical atmosphere. Leading a group of 30 students places extra pressure on the student teacher to manage the class; a smaller group might also decrease the likelihood that students would refer to the adults present when asking for advice and help.

Again, Mark's role was made more difficult because he was teaching his peers. He would have commanded greater authority with a younger age group. Indeed, it has been suggested (Rudduck and Flutter, 2004) that 'the optimum age gap is two or three years'. We resolved to ensure that any future sessions involving students as tutors would bring together an older student teacher and a younger group.

Jason

The other student teacher was Jason, who was designated as having special needs (dyslexia and attention deficit tendencies, together with hearing problems). He had, however, shown signs of high achievement and interest in aspects of Art. Jason was observed throughout a typical school day; we focused on his behaviour and attitude during lessons, to see whether these altered during the day and/or according to what teachers expected of him. The nature of the interactions between himself and his peers was also noted, with particular reference to the impact of his behaviour on them. We wanted to find out if he had a positive or negative leadership role.

Additionally, where possible, we sought information and advice from both teachers and learning support assistants (LSAs) who had experiences of teaching Jason. All relevant teachers were notified that he would be shadowed during the day. Jason was not told about the exercise, but he almost instantly recognised that he was the subject of the shadowing. Within the school, there is strong concern about his behaviour and attitude in classes and he is extremely conscious of this. This contrasts significantly with the reaction of Mark, who, although aware that an observation was taking place, did not make a personal connection.

This level of self-consciousness seemed to underpin Jason's behaviour throughout the day. His attention span was extremely short in all lessons and he spent a significant proportion of the lessons off-task. However, it became clear that he would often attempt to appear to be working when he was aware of being observed, but on closer inspection would have made only an initial start on the task and then started to doodle. Through this strategy he avoided close attention and any disciplinary action from the teacher. Teachers and support staff were aware of this; he was described as being despondent, easily off focus, and not appearing to care. In the larger group he seemed to exhibit low self-esteem and was at times defensive – answering his teachers back or mumbling a response. In all lessons, throughout the day, he was sitting at the rear of the classroom, a position that supported off-task behaviour. It is important to highlight here that Jason has hearing difficulties, and therefore may experience problems in a large classroom, especially when sitting at the back.

When working in a smaller group, his attention span was longer and his contribution to the group was greater. Within large groups, Jason did not contribute voluntarily. In contrast, within a small group of five in an English class, Jason was encouraged by the LSA and made frequent contributions; he demonstrated self-confidence when discussing the progress of a poster design he was developing within the English lesson. The LSA used his design as an example and flagged up his achievement in the task. She encouraged him to discuss his artwork, asking if Art was a subject he enjoyed. He reacted extremely positively to the praise and replied that he very much enjoyed Art and went on to describe the current art project he was undertaking in school.

In his next lesson, following a mid-morning break, when Jason had been playing football, his attitude towards his teacher noticeably worsened. He almost immediately challenged the male teacher, who was a few minutes late, and became verbally disruptive. As a result, he was asked to leave the classroom and stand outside the door. All interaction with the teacher had been negative, and Jason appeared to expect this response. Within this particular group, Jason exercised a more negative leadership role among his peers, suggesting that he was not committed to learning. He played to the crowd, living up to the expectation of both the teacher and other students. At this point, an incident occurred in the school. A fire alarm was smashed next to where Jason was standing; it turned out to be a false alarm but resulted in a whole school fire drill (the second that day). Jason, along with another boy, was questioned about the incident.

This had an effect on Jason throughout the remainder of the day, as other students were keen to discuss the incident with him, and he was equally keen to respond. Although Jason was not subsequently disciplined for this incident (whereas the other boy questioned was), students held an expectation at the time that Jason must have been to blame. Indeed, Jason said later in the day that although he didn't do it, everyone thought that he had.

Later in the day, a teacher who was aware that Jason was the subject of the observation described her experiences of teaching Jason to Diane, within earshot of Jason and several other students. Jason seemed unsurprised by the comments made about his lack of attention. However, these comments relate only to Jason's behaviour as a school student; no mention was made of his sense of humour nor of his creativity. His insecurity with many aspects of school culture in fact only becomes troublesome when it shows itself in challenging authority and it is, not surprisingly perhaps, the more negative and oppositional dimensions of his social interactions, not the positive ones, that feature most prominently in people's perceptions of Jason.

I had first met Jason when he was in Year 9. It is a measure of his reputation in the school that when I said to his teachers that I wanted to work with him in the classroom they saw it as a kind of baptism by fire for me, and appeared to take an almost gleeful delight in the prospect of my having to deal with him. However, as it turned out, although he was rather shy at first, he warmed to the idea of being special and leading a class in learning about graffiti. Jason had previously expressed an interest in graffiti art and, as a kind of ice-breaker, I showed him ways of drawing cartoons and some graffiti styles. He was initially interested but as the implications of the project dawned upon him, he became reluctant to commit himself. I arranged to supply him with some materials and books and he gradually became more involved; he was especially looking forward to taking on a leadership role. It is interesting to note that when we wrote to parents asking for permission to work with their children on this project, Jason's mother expressed the opinion that Jason would not be up to it; it was therefore not surprising that he seemed to lack confidence. Jason's self-esteem was based on having a reputation for being 'difficult' in class.

In Art, Jason tended to attain an average level of achievement in class, but he regularly failed to complete and submit homework. He became easily distracted and bored during most lessons. Consequently, he was often monitored closely throughout the lesson and required constant refocusing. However, during one lesson where the students were required to make a design to decorate a ceramic pot, he showed an eagerness to tessellate a motif using ICT. This activity was offered to the group as an alternative method of developing their design. He was on task through the lesson and succeeded in producing a strong outcome for his design. He expressed interest in working with ICT again, as he had access to a suitable ICT package at home. In later lessons, the group used images of fairground rides to investigate movement and speed, linking to the work of Futurists. Jason was fairly motivated by this theme, especially as he had the opportunity to incorporate some designs based upon graffiti styles.

Planning the teaching episode

I did not have the opportunity to pursue this initial contact with Jason as he was suspended from school before he had planned his teaching episode. However, as he had opted to continue to study Art in Year 10, I was able to follow up his progress during the next academic year and see how he could develop as a positive leader. My next meeting with him was by accident: on a school visit to discuss the progress of the project, I witnessed him being told off in the corridor. It was obvious that he had been sent out of the classroom. At break time, I stopped him in the corridor, saying 'Remember me? We were doing some graffiti designs together last year'. He seemed quite pleased and offered to show me some of his work in a sketchbook. It appeared that we were on course to do some more work for the project, despite his continuing track record of negative attitude towards many aspects of school.

I met Jason again a couple of weeks later and we talked about the possibility of his teaching a group of younger students. Prior to this, I observed him in his Art class, noting that he appeared to be disengaged from the class, not listening to the teacher, but absorbed in his own artwork, which was based on graffiti-style designs. After discussing ideas with other students and with the head of Art, it was agreed that Jason should do a kind of 'masterclass' in graffiti design with an after-school Art club for Year 7 students. Bearing in mind what we had learned by working with Mark earlier, we began to plan an activity involving Jason in a positive leadership role. By identifying his strengths and using these as a starting point, much might be achieved.

Graffiti is seen as an antisocial phenomenon and indeed it can often be so; I am not concerned here with trying to make a case for it being 'art'. Graffiti is often studiedly aggressive and would lose its reason for being if it were not done on other people's or public property. It is the fact that time and effort and consequent skill is involved which makes graffiti worthy of our attention in this context.

Although Jason was interested in graffiti and had expressed a willingness to be involved with teaching others, he appeared to have little awareness of the need to plan, or to practise his painting and designing skills for a particular audience. I was more worried about the possibility of a disastrous lesson than he appeared to be, and I seriously considered calling a halt. Jason was clearly nervous about the prospect of teaching others and continued to be ambivalent about the project for some time, largely, I believe because he was not fully confident in his ability. This was someone whose self-esteem was derived from negative (in school terms) behaviour and who was now trying to succeed in a task which for him had the potential to confirm his self-doubt. The teaching episode could be an opportunity for Jason to demonstrate positive leadership qualities and to succeed or it could prove to be another opportunity to demonstrate failure. On balance, I thought that Jason might benefit educationally from the experience and I decided that we should go ahead.

The teaching episode – and afterwards

Before the session, there were signs of nerves – beads of sweat on his forehead and a reddening around his neck, but these were hidden by the hood which he had decided to wear for the occasion. He wandered nervously around the room checking that everything was in order. His group of learners dribbled into the Art room with varying degrees of anticipation and amusement. Jason adopted a teacherish mode and stiffened his stance.

He started falteringly enough but soon gained confidence. As his group of learners became involved in the activity, he adopted his own teaching style – one which combined a gentle authority with a genuine empathy and concern for his students. They spent the session producing graffiti-style designs, using templates and experimenting with colour mixing, using spray paint. Jason's confidence grew, especially when his young learners were beginning to produce designs.

I caught up again with Jason a week or so later. Depressingly, he had to be summoned from the 'isolation room' – a recent innovation in the school – where miscreants could be isolated from the rest of the school community and be observed by closed circuit cameras.

Reflecting upon the session, Jason felt that it went 'all right', despite his initial nervousness. He seemed to have gained in self-esteem, but more importantly, I felt that he had developed a greater empathy for others. He spoke of how he had more respect for, or at least sympathy with, teachers. He said that teaching was 'hard, but you get used to it' and that forward planning for lessons was essential. I asked him what he liked and did not like about school and what he would change if he could. He said he liked being in the Art room because 'I can get on with work and talk at the same time'. He did not like it when teachers in other subjects 'have a go at you for nothing'. As for changing the school, top of his list was 'get rid of the isolation room'; he added that this would not happen because 'I don't think they would listen'. He was then escorted back to the isolation room.

Jason was often absent, 'in trouble' or suspended from school when we wanted to work with him on this project. But from my own observations and from what he himself said about his experience of being part of the project, it seems that his confidence grew as a result of taking on a teaching role with a younger group and he was less disengaged. What the project was not able to do was to spend more time in the school to help sustain the changes.

'Now I stop and think before I do something stupid'

Morgan, Brian, Rachel and Tyson are 12 going on 13, well established in Year 8 and in the same class for most things. Despite the school's 'boy-next-to-girl' seating policy, Morgan and Rachel sometimes manage to sit next to each other, Brian and Tyson never: as Brian says, 'It doesn't take much to set us off'. For all four, along with the rest of their class, the novelty of the new school in Year 7 has worn off and Year 8 has become the much documented limbo world (see Rudduck and Flutter, 2004). Like the rest of their class they are uncertain about the purpose of their schooling. However, their minds are concentrated on their school's finely tuned system of rewards and punishments and this is at the forefront of their concerns about school and the source of what appear to be daily injustices. They know that they should believe that in their school 'It is cool to achieve.' And they know about 'the right to teach – the right to learn', for this moral principle is to be read at the front of every classroom. As I came to share in their understandings I realised that making connections with moral principles was not an easy task. Their moral way was, rather, an uncomplicated search for goodness and mutuality as found in relationships with each other, and with some of their teachers.

Their tutor group, which is the basis for most of their teaching groups, is a lively one. The start of each day is tutorial time, a buzz of social clatter making a transitional space between home and school. There are groups of twos and threes as well as larger clusters distinguishable by gender, class and commitment to schooling. There is the cross-chat about last evening's missed call on the mobile phone, the harsh bonding jibes between boys, the comments that hurt made to the two outsiders, and the gently exercised pastoral care of their tutor.

Their tutor, a teacher of five years' standing, speaks of the group as being a handful before Christmas: disorientated and losing the plot. Their Science teacher talks of needing to impose a tough regime of drills and a 'persistent and insistent' approach, and their Art teacher sees the class as 'an interesting bunch. I never know how they are going to be. You have some sessions with them when you think, "Shall I give up teaching? Am I professionally incompetent?"' For their Music teacher, the class is a typical Year 8 group: an interesting mix, with its fair share of characters.

Making sense

Art, along with Drama, Music and PE, features strongly in the four students' preferred list of school subjects. They like doing things. They like the process of making and celebrating what they have made, they like to make connections, see how things fit together. In these respects, it is Expressive Arts subjects that most obviously enable the class to gather meaning and purpose and build confidence. Expressive Arts teachers are encouraging, observes Brian, and goes on to explain that they have to be, for how else would students risk expressing themselves, committing their ideas and feelings to public scrutiny?

Their school teaches students to be aware of and make use of their many intelligences and most hold on to the discovery that they are 'body smart'. But for Brian this is rather more than the usual cognitive construct. Brian tells of a more complex and richer notion, with the body providing a source of agency and identity:

> Your body can show how you are thinking, what you are thinking, the way you are quite basically, the person you are... Things like Music can help express that. It's just a way of getting it out of your body. Most lessons you're just sitting down. You're just sitting down answering questions out of a textbook. And really kids of our age prefer to be doing something else. Practising something on the keyboard like we do in Music or something different like in Drama. Acting out. I suppose Art's different even though it's still on paper, because it's still another expression. I suppose that's why they are called Expressive Arts. We had a brilliant lesson on Wednesday in Art. We are all doing a God-like creature that you'd find in a jungle. I did a tiger, orange and black lines. So it looked like a tiger with red eyes and everything. It was really good. I thought so.

Opportunities like this are in stark contrast to the lessons that are a matter of exposition and practice, where students feel they have insufficient support and where there is little space to bring something of themselves to the learning. They like the curriculum to have human interest. For example:

- finding out about homeless children in Life Skills Lessons
- the wonders of human reproduction in Science
- the invitation to bring to school what they know about Italy (and many know a lot through parents and grandparents)
- the telling of stories about people in History

- the human rights poem in Humanities.

These all lead to times when curriculum content raises interest and commitment. Above all else, they want teachers to 'make connections with them', to have 'teachers who understand things', for this is how it was in primary school. Tyson recalls the secure world of the primary school and contrasts it to the impersonal world of secondary school and his search for trusting relationships:

> Primary teachers were interested in you, knew which television programmes you watched, which football team you supported. You could have a joke with them. I liked the chat at the end of the day making everything feel all right. There are too many systems and procedures in secondary school. We've been knuckled down and it still doesn't change a lot of people. Some teachers when we don't understand blame it on you. We learn when we can talk about it, discuss it. Life Skills is good. The teacher talks with you as if you were mature and you feel OK. Everybody loved their Primary teacher. Teachers in secondary school need to trust us more.

For Tyson, as for many of his class, the transition from primary to secondary school has proved difficult. In a year group of 250 students, the head of year identifies 25 per cent who have not settled well and who have become to some extent problematic or disaffected. Tyson receives his fair share of negative points, occasional detention as well as commendations. Tyson's form tutor views him as being always pleasant and polite, very sociable and liked and he has been elected as tutor representative on the Year 8 student council. However, his tutor notes that he is slow to take responsibility for his own behaviour. Other teachers tell more:

> ... amiable and good on the surface, but very disruptive [...] has difficulty in accepting authority [...] others do look up to him, some through fear rather than respect [...] loses concentration easily and gives up if he feels the work is difficult [...] enjoys being at the centre and the one to whom others defer [...] probably the strongest personality in the group, he is an intelligent boy.

The head of year has a 'top 20' list of troublesome students, cases that the system regularly refer to him. Of Tyson, Rachel, Morgan and Brian, it is Brian who has hit the top 20 in Year 8 and his teachers view him as problematic:

… a boy whose tactics are very covert and one who is adept at putting the responsibility onto someone else; one who can be malicious with words and who enjoys winding people up … easily distracts others, stirring them to misdeeds and who does not respect the right to teach and learn. Brian is always not on task.

However, Brian is thoughtful about how school is working for him and his contemporaries. He tells of a school that is in two parts: one is a school heavily dependent upon the use of sticks and carrots, and one is a school where for some you get caught in-between, a school that is difficult to access:

I actually feel that school has grown to be the way it is now because of being threatened with detentions, being rewarded with commendations. Everyone has split themselves by their own frame of mind into those who say, 'I want to be good. I want to get commendations. I want to get rewards. I want to get stuff.' Other people, they know this is hard and it's so much easier to fall below standard. Then you get a bad reputation and there's no chance to redeem yourself. Teachers work on reputations. It splits people, it splits the school.

A lesson with a difference

I first encountered the class of Morgan, Brian, Rachel and Tyson for their Friday Music Lesson, a lesson I observed each week during the second and third terms of Year 8. After each lesson I talked with and consulted members of the class. I observed the class in a variety of other lessons too. This is how I came to know the class and their perceptions of schooling and where I came to know Morgan, Rachel, Tyson and Brian.

Brian views Friday as a good day and there is the Music lesson to look forward to:

Music is a big change from the rest of the lessons. It puts you in a different frame of mind. I definitely think music is a big influence. It can alter the way you think. Very quickly and easily. Just by simply listening to a piece of music. Change the way you think. When we say we have Music next we say it with a happy voice.

Their Music teacher is much respected. He is seen as knowing what he is doing; he 'understands things. He is a Peter Pan with intelligence'. In Music, the class attends to their teacher and to each other, learning how music is to be created. Before the end of the lesson they will be performing something they have created themselves and that has never before existed and they will be valuing each other's endeavours. They will know what it is to improvise and compose music, to become informed musical critics and to reflect upon their musical tastes and preferences. Their teacher will connect with them and touch their core concerns and convince them that whatever they are asked to do can be done:

> Yes, you can do it, you really can. You will surprise yourself. Go on, you can do it. Just have a go and use your ears.

Music lessons are not a place where negative points and detentions are gained, rather a place where those on report are sympathetically dealt with and where all are encouraged to feel good. Students learn to acknowledge when they are not doing their best or working for the common good.

Today is the first Music lesson after the Christmas holidays. Morgan sits alongside Rachel with a passive gaze and I feel that there is a deep detachment here. Morgan tells me later:

> I don't like me. I live in two houses. I wouldn't come to school unless I had to. If the teacher isn't strict I don't bother, just chat. There have been 21 members of my family who have been to this school and they have all made bad tracks. My mum is worried how my brother will get on when he comes up to the school in September.

Morgan is widely viewed in negative terms by her teachers:

> Morgan, no motivation, no ambition ... drifting ... distracts others ... very talkative ... sits at the front yet is easily sidetracked ... subtle negative leadership ... gives up if she feels the work is too difficult ... can be very negative as a way of maintaining authority over others.

Another teacher views her as a 'helpless learner', lacking in any initiative, and this he feels is a characteristic of many students in the school. Morgan values those of her teachers who find a humane way into learning and this will involve informal talk at the beginning of lessons and the possibility of sharing life experiences – the discussion of a recent bereavement, for example.

How people live their daily lives intrigues Morgan and Religious Studies and History can capture her interest. She has always loved stories in History. She said:

> Good teachers listen, know what to do, keep pupils occupied. But many talk too much and don't listen.

Today, Morgan's Music teacher draws her into the lesson, asking her to come to the front of the class to demonstrate the new skill being learned. As she does this, Rachel, Brian and Tyson, like the rest of the class, watch with rapt attention. Will they be asked too? Tyson is always ready to come to the front and if it is a case of volunteers, his hand will be up first. Tyson is the showman, like his favourite uncle whose athletic prowess he much admires and whom he looks forward to visiting, for then he will learn new moves on the large trampoline as well as the odd circus trick.

Brian has already contributed to the lesson in the opening discussion about the kinds of sounds made in the music of North India played as the class entered the Music room. Brian thought the sitar sounded like a didgeridoo, but then he would, for his recent trip to Australia is at the front of his mind.

Rachel, sitting next to Morgan will, in due course, have her turn at the front of the Music class showing how things might be and here I am her keyboard partner. Rachel is a twin and has had difficulties with her speech, but is in the top set for Maths and loves to dance. For Rachel, it is her youthful auntie, once a ballroom champion, that inspires her. Her teachers find a number of negative qualities in Rachel's approach to lessons:

> Rachel, attentive but often seems to be at the centre of some issue with other students, with some much more high-profile agitators within the group ... prone to arguing with her peers ... poor attitude ... on occasions refuses to work with other students ... the quiet one who works with Morgan to divert the lesson plan.

Unschooled music

Morgan, Rachel, Tyson and Brian are stilled by their Music lesson, and value being taught by a teacher who doesn't get stressed. They go to lunch at ease with themselves and with their school, or perhaps it is just Friday. None of the four have had formal musical instruction in or out of school but music is playing a significant part in their lives. Their out-of-school Music curriculum involves listen-move-sing, with a good balance between learning that is both planned for and casual. Most obviously this out-of-school curriculum is called upon immediately after school, as they find another space in which to make the necessary adjustment between school and home life. Rachel, like Morgan, dances for as much as two hours with the help of a karaoke machine, while Brian and Tyson move between their Justin Timberlake body waves, BMX biking and football. Brian has a guitar and is beginning to pick out rhythmic riffs as he listens to his mini-disc, something he has learned to do in his school Music lessons, and Tyson has recently retrieved his keyboard from the loft. For all four, Justin Timberlake is their man and '*Justified*' their album.

All this is a private engagement with music, providing the necessary antidote to the experience of school with its fraught relationships, unsatisfying promiscuities and the treadmill of anxiety and boredom. Morgan, alone of the four, is learning music in a public space beyond school. For two and a half hours each Friday evening it is Morgan's time to be a Majorette. This involves missing the television soap, *EastEnders*. There is more than a hint that the time is coming to move on from majoretting, for all the badges and medals have been gained, but preparation is in hand for a national competition and that presents a reason for carrying on.

My observation of Tyson's impromptu body waves as he enters his Music classroom to the music of Justin Timberlake provides a cue to begin the process of selection and form the group that will be offered the challenge of taking on curriculum leadership through the use of their unschooled musical talents. The Music teacher agrees that Tyson would be a good choice, and someone in the class who responds to careful nurture. Brian seemed to be a good choice too, someone who was insightful about his difficulties with classroom learning and who, like Tyson, is a body-waving skateboarder. I proposed Morgan, knowing of her majoretting skill and detachment from schooling. The Music teacher added Rachel as a student with talent in dance and whose verbal capability limited success in some curriculum areas and who appeared to be low in confidence.

We were now ready to invite Morgan, Tyson, Rachel and Brian to design a teaching episode for another class in their school, making use of their talents developed through their out-of-school engagement with music. Their desire to be valued for who they are and for what they have to offer, and to be treated as responsible would now be tested. They were about to be asked to undertake a challenge that they least expected from their school.

Becoming teachers

The students were surprised by the invitation to become teachers. There was initial diffidence and while Morgan and Rachel were quick to acknowledge their majoretting and dancing prowess, Tyson and Brian were less sure about their talents – concern about how they wished to present themselves came to the fore. My suggestion that Tyson and Brian were skilled body wavers was deflected into their perceived potential as guitarists, keyboardists and drummers. However, they had come on board and agreed to meet weekly to plan what they would teach and how they might teach it to a class in Year 7. Meetings were convened and their Music teacher maintained a log.

At the first meeting, the leaders reviewed their talents with support from their Music teacher and myself. We agreed that Tyson learns things quickly on the keyboard (this week, he had learned 'Mission Impossible' and managed to teach another member of his class during the Music lesson). He likes to play the drums too but above all else is a whiz with the Michael Jackson shuffle. Rachel dances a lot at home, Morgan is brilliant at baton twirling and dancing and Brian is a dab hand at guitar and, of course, a good dancer too. The group became convinced that they could work on a routine that involved twirling, a dance, the guitar and keyboard. (The boys' body wave and shuffle remained on hold.)

An early decision was to use the Justin Timberlake song, *Like I Love You*. The music, a fusion of soul and punk, advertised as deferring to the worlds of Stevie Wonder and Michael Jackson and with distinctive riffs and pervasive rhythms, was considered ideal; it was easy to dance to and move to. The student teachers viewed Justin Timberlake as the new Michael Jackson and his music would be familiar to all those taught.

The four were provided with a space and tape recorder and asked to document progress through an audio diary. If the leaders felt they had come up with something significant they would stop working and make an audio note. Enthusiasm was growing as they pointed out that one lesson would be insufficient. A sequence of three lessons would be needed. An intuitive grasp of structure and wholeness of experience was quick to emerge. Morgan led the case for beginning with demonstration, with a modelling of the skills to be learned, and the presentation of a clear vision of what might be achieved. This proposal met with a counter proposal from Tyson who made the case for holding back the whole picture.

Their discussions were a subtle analysis of, and sometimes explicit enquiry into, the methods and strategies adopted by their best teachers that made sense for them as learners – and also what it was that alienated them as learners. The group decided on an opening performance to engage, although they realised that this would be a considerable challenge and serious risk. Brian and Tyson had by now resolved to share their body waving talents. They were engaged in a creative process and wanted to make something special. They had established a 'holding form' and now the messy, hard graft of moving from the vision to actualities had begun.

It was time to draw from the student teachers their purpose. They provided not an instructional objective but a procedural one linked to pedagogy:

> We want to get the whole class to perform, in small groups, our special out-of-school skills and abilities, and to put these together in a final performance. We want them to find new ways of responding to music. We will teach by showing, helping individuals, encouraging, [we will] give slight cues, praise, make it interesting, humour, introduce music, give certificates for taking part. We need to think about how our favourite teachers teach and maybe use their ideas. We can play some calming music, something they know and like. We can give commendations – Year 7s like commendations. We can give certificates to everybody for just taking part – we should not just give them to the best.

The four became clear that their opening performance would need to inspire, that there should be scope for choice of activity and that each of them would work with a group of about eight students before drawing the class together. Uppermost in their minds was the need to engage their charges from the outset. They were determined that all learners would succeed and that the sequence of lessons would end in celebration. This would take the form of a final performance by each group showing, in a climate of mutual respect, what had been learned.

The discussion frequently centred on ways of rewarding the students' achievements and it was agreed that all would receive a participatory certificate, and that there would also be a learners' consensus through which the best group would receive particular acclaim. From the student teachers' perspective, three criteria for success would be addressed. There would be:

- the valuing of positive attitude, commitment and a willingness to help others

- recognition of the most accomplished performance

- recognition of the group that showed most spirit.

Meetings continued with reasonable regularity but there were to be continuous disruptions to the process and it proved difficult to find times when all four were present. One week Rachel was not available as she was excluded for fighting. Rachel's absence promoted Morgan's disengagement and then her majoretting equipment was left at home. Then there was Brian's holiday in Lanzarote, Morgan's absence during the last week of term and Brian excluded from lessons for accumulating ten negative points (he was taken out of rehearsal by a senior member of staff). On this occasion, Brian's behaviour had been consistently bad in every subject except Music. And then there was Tyson's internal exclusion when he wrote on the school's mid-year review form that 'teachers in this school don't know how to teach'. At times, sustaining the project was difficult. The commitment of their Music teacher and support from the headteacher were crucial.

As the planning progressed, so were there times of serious self-doubt amongst the four, concerns about street-credibility and the obvious fear of failure. Tyson's lapses in confidence were most noticeable and here Brian took on the role of mentor to Tyson and also exercised a subtle leadership role within the group. Brian reassured Tyson that he would support him and make sure he succeeded. Their Music teacher noted that:

> *Brian is working as a skilful teacher. He is reassuring and initiating a joint professional journey where there is no superior–inferior relationship. He is very encouraging, supportive to his friend. Here is a student who can be a 'tricky customer' in certain lessons working in a very sensitive way with another 'tricky customer'. It is good to have Brian on board. He is particularly perceptive, artistic. Would Brian's skill come more to the fore if the school arts culture was a true microcosm of the students' home or street culture?*

As time for action approached, so the student teachers suggested that it would be helpful if they could observe the Year 7 class they were going to work with.

This was to be a salutary experience, as their reflections show:

> They were a naughty class, only a handful looked as if they were listening, might be difficult to teach them ... Linda is naughty ... what if we played the music when they came into the classroom ... what if we rewarded them with commendations ... I think they would listen once we started teaching them because it was interesting ... I think that I would bop them if they played up.

Now the leaders saw the challenge as one of turning the class around. They knew that they would need to engage the class throughout and develop positive attitudes. The experience had to be a good one. The event had to be memorable. There was no room for failure.

Teaching and learning

The venue chosen was a softly-lit dance studio, a warm space inviting performance intimacy. The Year 7 class entered expectantly and sat in two prepared rows and without a word the jagged yet softly arresting riff from Justin Timberlake's 'Like I Love You' brought on the dance and majoretting of Rachel and Morgan, and then Brian and Tyson presented a dialogue of mime and movement. The audience were intrigued, remained attentive throughout and at the end applauded. A gauche explanation followed from Tyson. Each then worked with a group of eight students modelling their skills to the track, 'Cry me a river'. There followed coaching and a process of continual nurture. Each group showed what they had done, a move that the leaders believed would ensure consolidation of learning, in the statutory plenary. The class left for their next lesson. The student teachers were elated.

> It makes you think on your feet. I like my group. They were really good ... They were doing their own thing ... Linda was on task! ... We played the music and it calmed them down right away ... It makes you appreciate what a teacher has to do. Teachers need lesson plans ... Everybody seemed to have enjoyed it. It's not a big thing any more.

The second lesson a week later saw the four encouraging students to develop their own ideas, transforming the material offered in the previous session. As before, a plenary to consolidate progress brought the session to an end:

> They needed my input at certain times ... They were learning how
> to respond to the changes in the music ... The students followed
> instructions easily ... It was easy to use their ideas.

The third session allowed the learners to polish what they had produced in preparation for the final performance. Final performance time arrived and took the form of an act of celebration incorporating the much considered certification of achievement for all students and a special award for the most successful group, decided upon by the whole class. Tyson concluded the event with a short thank you speech:

> Thanks very much for taking part in this project and helping us to
> help you. You've been really good in behaviour and practicals and
> every one of you were good. I hope you enjoyed it as much as
> I did.

From the questionnaire given to all members of the class taught, 97 per cent thought the standard of teaching in the three lessons was 'good' or 'very good' and 90 per cent that the teaching had helped them to be 'creative' or 'very creative'. These were some of the Year 7s' comments:

> Morgan was very positive and helpful ... she showed me clearly
> what to do ... taught me how to baton twirl ... she showed me
> first and then I go off and do it by myself and if I got it wrong
> Morgan would help me.

> Rachel helped me by showing me how to do the dance moves
> easily, she repeated the moves to make it easier ... Rachel got to
> know me and was very pleasant about explaining the task ... she
> showed me clearly what I had to do ... she supported us ... she
> encouraged us and joined in with us.

> Tyson showed us what to do and how to do it ... he had
> confidence in us ... he said, 'You can do it.'

> Brian was understanding and he helped us all the time even if we
> couldn't do it and he always said we were the best ... he gave us
> confidence ... he asked us what we wanted to do.

In open discussion there was appreciation of the way their ideas had been used and students repeatedly spoke of how their learning had been supported and how the student teachers had encouraged them; if they didn't get it right they were helped to get it right. It was fun and interesting and by being 'dancical' they had come to know the music really well. They had learned to listen carefully. The music had been an inspiring choice:

> Listening to people like Justin Timberlake and Eminem means you can feel like them and feeling like somebody else feels helps a lot, especially if things have happened in their life that are happening to you. It's good to feel like Justin Timberlake. We need models and heroes.

There was appreciation of the way the student teachers had communicated, using not too many words – and their words – and movement. All this was contrasted to their experience in many of their school lessons. There was a strongly held view that their teachers talk at them too much – talk to themselves really and don't allow enough time to do the work. A member of the class spoke of the routine of being asked for ideas only for them to discover that the teacher always had the best idea. And here the students returned to the Expressive Arts curriculum that they experienced in school:

> In Expressive Arts you can express your personality ... you can be really creative without anybody telling you it's wrong ... in Art they don't tell you how to move your hand ... you can tell people a message through your drawing and music ... in Expressive Arts you can show your talent ... Expressive Arts is about working together, it teaches you to work as a team ... if there is somebody who can't do it we help them.

For one Y7 student the whole experience was like a game of Jenga. Jenga was a game well known to all the students and involves either building or dismantling a tower made of wooden blocks. The task is to avoid making the tower fall. The objective is to be the last player to stack or dismantle a block without knocking the tower over. Interestingly, the Y7 students viewed the game as collaborative. Matt explained:

> They gave us a piece of the puzzle, a starting point and we built on it ... in Jenga you have to work together ... you don't want to let anybody else down ... you have to concentrate to do what you need to do ... you have to agree on the moves. If somebody is doing it wrong, you have to help them out, not shout at them. You have to support.

For Emily, the making of a jigsaw came to mind. She was especially impressed by the group's presentation at the outset. This had been inspiring and it was like seeing the whole jigsaw, the jigsaw that they were going to make together:

> The four leaders became the corners of the puzzle and we all filled it in so that by the third lesson it was ready to be seen. It was a pretty picture.

Doing something useful

The project's culmination was in the final weeks of the summer term. This meant that the school year had ended positively for Morgan, Tyson, Rachel and Brian. As the project had developed, so Tyson volunteered to assist with the school production of Bugsy Malone and in the event played the part of a Boxer. His short, carefully crafted mime in the ring was impressive. In his end-of-year assembly, he gained three awards and was taken out for a meal that evening by his parents. Morgan is still talking about giving up majorettes and Rachel has not been in any more fights. Brian's form tutor is speaking positively of Brian's attitude. His head is high and he is giving winks, nods and smiles. It was Brian who had most to say about the experience of teaching others:

> I thought it would be tougher than it was. I thought it would be a bit more of a struggle. I thought that they might not cooperate as much as they did, that they wouldn't be enjoying it so much. I thought that they might not be bothering to do it. 'Let's not do it, let's be stupid.' They helped me in a way as well as me helping them.
>
> All the times we had off from lessons practising, we were doing something useful. If we had been in lessons, we would probably just've been messing around. Just not doing anything at all, not learning anything new, not using ourselves for anything useful, decent. But then we got the time off to practise getting better at something.
>
> We want to keep involved in all this. We don't want to let it go. I feel more positive about school insofar as you can understand the teachers. We taught three times in two weeks not five times a day, five days a week. That must be tough, harder than we appreciate. You can understand why they get frustrated so easily, which makes you better towards them. My attitude in class has

definitely improved. We learned how it feels if nobody is going to cooperate [and] how to make them quiet without going over the top. I think I am a much better judge of what good teaching is now. Good teachers make sure their students are happy, at ease with what they are doing. They let their students have ideas. They are fair. They don't work on reputations. It's a shame to be back on full timetable.

I definitely feel more confident towards the class, but I am not sure about more generally. I feel more confident about standing up in front of people as a group. You are not going to get up and dance in Maths. I really don't think there is any way Maths lessons can be made interesting. I feel more adult and would like to have more responsibility. ... Now I stop and think before I do something stupid. That's taking more responsibility. I feel I want to help my teachers more. I have tried to impress them but they haven't noticed I'm different.

Sustaining it

While short-term effects were positive and encouraging, sustaining them proved to be difficult.

Their Music teacher was fully aware of how the four had changed as a result of their experience as student teachers. He had changed his teaching approach to reflect his determination not to underestimate young people and what they understand and can do. He tried to build on the positive experience of 'the four' by nominating them as 'lead learners'. He said he valued having come to know them as responsible young adults. In interview, he reflects too on the structures of schooling that make it difficult to change colleagues' perceptions of the status of students and that prevent the students' voices from being heard:

I see them now as more confident, more strident. They seem to understand a lot more. They seem empowered, almost with another knowledge. I've spoken to them so many times about different things and, these days, it is an interaction rather than an adult speaking to a young person who responds when spoken to. They say that they understand teachers a lot more. And whether they understand me a bit more, I don't know, but this understanding seems to have given them the power to talk to me on an even footing. I have begun to understand what they can and cannot do – well, there is no 'cannot' at the moment.

This project has helped me to understand that there is a lot more to these pupils, in fact to all young people. It has affected the way I teach, the way I plan my lessons. I use the idea of 'lead learners' a lot. I have pretty much done that before by strategically choosing more able students, or even less able students to model or scaffold an idea or activity. Now I think more consciously about the disaffected students when choosing models. I ask the students how they want to learn. 'What is the problem with the way we have done that? Shall we try it your way? What is your way?' They will always tell me.

This boldly challenges a philosophy that many of my colleagues expound and that is that we have to spoon-feed the students. 'We have to lead them by the nose even in Year 10 and 11.' This idea irritates me so much. No wonder they misbehave! Our student researchers challenge this directly. They have their self-respect and knowledge to share with each other and us, with some help of course.

I tended to think that I am the artist, the resource, that I am the live music maker. Now, however, I am seeing the whole class as the resource. Each class is a dynamic resource. I look for this every hour that I teach. I am now thinking about ways forward for schools. I would love to change the culture of teachers. I would love to be part of something that changes teachers' perceptions of how to teach and how to learn, and above all, how they might regard their students. It would be good to see a culture change in the school.

One of my appraisal targets is to disseminate what is being learnt from this project. I have presented our findings to various teams and individuals. While the management are interested, this is where it stops. I don't think my colleagues are willing to go the whole way and make radical changes. They acknowledge there is a problem. The management put new systems in place, they rejuvenate old ones but there is nothing wrong with the systems that we already have. It is our perception of the students, that's what we've got to change. It might take a long time.

Even though the students had demonstrated their capacity to take on responsibility, grow skilfully as teachers, declare a deepening empathy with their own teachers and with those they taught, reputations in school were hard to change. While they were now making an effort to engage and learn in other subjects and with teachers who had not always made it easy for them, their past reputations held firm in teachers' minds and were reflected in their written reports. Attention was still being drawn to their old deficits and their attempts to be different went unnoticed by many of their teachers. For instance, the targets teachers gave Tyson reiterated the need to display a more positive attitude, to ensure total concentration, to complete homework and to develop a work ethic. Brian, although now well out of the 'top 20' trouble makers, was still being called upon to change his attitude, to concentrate one hundred per cent and ignore distractions and to realise that his behaviour was selfish. Morgan needed to find greater focus too and to discover self-motivation so that tasks could be completed. Only in Rachel's case was there evidence of her new effort being noticed: the perennial call for her to become more actively involved and more assertive in lessons now featured a little less than before.

There was evidence however that their experience as student teachers may have lifted their confidence and enabled them to raise their aspirations. For both Morgan and Rachel, options for the next stage of their schooling provided the opportunity to opt for Health and Social Care and they were enthused about this. Morgan's mother had even suggested a possible career as a child psychiatrist or a lawyer specialising in child abuse. Tyson and Brian became set on emigration to Canada and a world of professional Ice Hockey. And Brian remained as insightful and philosophical about school and life as ever:

> Year 7 and 8 just fly by. Year 9 feels like another school. I'm starting to understand things much better this year. People, cultures, things that happened in History and why they happened. Words mean something. In Year 7 you're too concerned to get friends. Now school is a great place to be, like one big social network. I can't wait for lunchtimes. It's bad to grow up with criticism – some do, but some grow up with encouragement. The way it is can affect your whole life. Being criticised all the time makes you look stupid. Being encouraged all the time makes you feel great.

Extending the opportunities

While short-term effects were positive and encouraging, sustaining them proved difficult. Indeed, it was easier to create opportunities for some sort of continuation beyond the school than to extend it within the school.

In this chapter, we focus on activities that the link researchers in two schools, with the support of the teachers, were able to develop. These activities served to strengthen the students' emerging confidence and responsibility – and they also confirmed our sense of the richness of their often hidden insights into the dynamics of social situations in the classroom.

The extension activities were only manageable in the two schools that were within reasonable travelling distance from our Cambridge base. Morag Morrison invited the two students she had worked with, Ashley and Kayleigh, to talk, in a question and answer format, with two groups of trainee teachers. The sessions were recorded and the dialogues transcribed. (Given the size of the room and the ambient noise levels, the recorder did not pick up everything and the transcript is therefore only a partial record.) John Finney set up three extension opportunities for the four Music 'student teachers': a session with trainee teachers, a session with Year 7 students in another secondary school and a session with Year 1 and 2 pupils in a local primary school. In all three sessions, the student teachers 'taught' their groups.

The two accounts are different in style and reflect the differences in data. The first ('Expert witnesses') offers a summary and analysis based on the transcripts of the two sessions with the trainee teachers. The second ('Intuitive practitioners') focuses on the session with the Y1 and Y2 pupils and includes extracts from a long commentary written by the primary teacher who observed the student teachers' session.

'Expert witnesses'

There were about 20 trainee teachers at each session; they sat in a circle with Ashley and Kayleigh positioned at a prominent place in the circle – ie, a rather exposed and potentially frightening arrangement. However, the two student teachers, although rather nervous at first, quickly got into the swing of things and were confident enough by the end of the first session to present alternative suggestions for dealing with really difficult situations in class. The trainee teachers sought their advice in all seriousness and regarded them as 'expert witnesses' on issues of classroom management.

The trainee teachers asked Ashley and Kayleigh a series of 'from the heart' questions, focusing first on their experiences as 'naughty pupils' and moving onto their experiences as 'student teachers'; they seemed increasingly ready to seek advice from the two girls and to respect their responses. Here are some of the questions put to the two girls:

- What did you get into the biggest trouble for?
- What are the things that teachers do that wind you up?
- What consequences (ie disciplinary responses) really bother you?
- Did you have any teachers that you actually respected, at all, ever?
- What motivates you? What makes you want to work?
- What sort of things did those Drama teachers say to you that was different to what other teachers say to you?
- How did you like coming up with the strategies to deal with the behaviour of the Year 6s or to get them to work, because obviously sometimes, like you said, they were mouthy and sometimes they were just unwilling to work?
- [If a teacher you usually like has shouted at you] how do you think the teacher can make it up to you?
- How can the teacher make a good impression if you've never met the teacher before, if you've got no relationship?
- Can you tell us something about the emotional side of teaching: how can you show that you're a real person without showing weaknesses? Is there anything you'd advise a teacher to do?
- If I've got three individuals that are completely ruining it for everybody else, what's your advice to me: What do I do with those other people? Do I make the whole class suffer? Do I send them out, do I speak to them, or do I give them written work to do?

The two girls were not hesitant in responding to questions about what they 'got into the biggest trouble for', nor were they brash or boastful but gave straightforward accounts:

> Walking out the classroom, not aggressive as in like I'd punch the teacher, but my tone of voice and stuff. And you don't think about it.

Without denying responsibility for their own actions, they acknowledged that 'certain things can trigger you off and set your hormones going'. For example:

- teachers shouting at you, or talking to you 'in that horrible tone'
- having to 'sit there for about seven minutes' with your hand up while they 'always go to someone else'
- teachers not being prepared to listen to your side of the story when you are excluded from the classroom
- teachers going on shooting questions at you to show everyone you are not paying attention
- getting picked on because of your reputation when everyone is guilty of mucking about.

They also dislike it when they heard teachers blaming their behaviour on their background:

> I hate it when people say to you it's their home life, it's their upbringing. It's not. It's your own, it's the way you're doing things.

They presented themselves as having changed and were asked what led to the change; their responses were unhesitating:

> I become a teacher [ie a student teacher] and I respect teachers more. And I respect their feelings and stuff as well.

Both girls talked about the way that teaching their own group had helped them to see things from the teacher's perspective. Before, they 'didn't think about teachers' feelings' but would 'just do it anyway', but now they think twice about behaving badly:

> Because you know what it's like and how far you can push teachers. And then you think, oh but when I [was teaching] look at when they done it to me; look how stressed I got. Then you feel quite guilty, don't you.

> I felt now I'd been teaching, the teachers, I felt quite disgusted with myself that I'd given them not that much respect.

The two girls revealed how good they were at analysing classroom interactions – explaining how disruption could escalate to involve the whole class and how students could quickly work together, mercilessly sometimes, to destabilise a teacher who seemed nervous:

> If they show to you that they're not that strong, then you can climb all over them. You know their weak point, you find out what that is and you'll keep doing it.

Again, there were signs of their own recent experiences as student teachers building a new empathy:

> And then, sometimes, you feel quite sorry because they look like they're just there on their own and you look at them and you think, aah ...

The girls also offered sensible advice about how to defuse tense situations. For example, they are clear that a teacher should not shout:

> I think the worst thing you can do to somebody, and you will not get their attention, is shouting at them. I know it's real hard for you not to shout at somebody. You get so stressed, but I don't think shouting does anything.

Nor should they try to argue with them in front of the class – or the others might join in the fun 'and then the group will get bigger and the battle will become worse and worse'. Instead, the teacher should ask the student to see them at the end of the day, somewhere private. The girls had little time for detentions which were not seen as a constructive response:

> You get took out of a lesson and you'll be sitting there for an hour doing nothing.

Instead, they favoured teachers talking things through with students and finding out **why** they were making trouble, and discussing what could be done to avoid such a situation in the future. They also suggested that teachers who lost control and shouted should explain what made them lose their cool:

> When they don't explain why they just shouted at you, you get really angry [and then] you'll want to wind them up for the rest of the day.

> Being able to have a dialogue was good because each of you could see where the other was coming from [...] and when you're both working together things get sorted out easier.

The trainee teachers became increasingly comfortable in describing situations which they didn't know how to respond to – such as when two students were being energetically disruptive. Here, the two girls disagreed, one suggesting that the teacher separate the miscreants and the other taking a different tack – but what was important was that the logic of the alternative responses was brought out and discussed.

The two girls reminded their audience that there was no one strategy that would work for every situation:

> There's not just one way you can handle all kids because everyone's different and different personalities. Like you can't be soft with all the children and you can't be hard with all the children. It's because some children have different personalities and you have to treat them in different ways.

Again, good advice, rooted in the realities of their own experience.

Although the questions were mostly about how teachers might respond to difficulties, some trainee teachers wanted to know more about the things that helped the two girls to focus positively on learning. They agreed that they preferred a climate in which they felt trusted and were praised:

> Praise does get me. I feel happy and I'm like, yeah, and I'll do more. It makes me feel happy about what I've done and I'm happy to work.

> I think the best reward is somebody telling you you've done well.

They said they wanted content that meant something to them, like 'real life things'. And they liked teachers to be relaxed, 'because when you know that a teacher's happy, they're cheerful and they're not moody, they're not stressy'. They want teachers to show that they care about the students and will ask them how they feel about things – 'for that puts me in gear and makes me think, "Oh, I actually had better start putting my head down and sorting it out"'.

The two sessions with the trainee teachers ended with spontaneous applause – they had got memorable advice, not from textbooks but straight, as it were, 'from the horse's mouth'.

Intuitive practitioners

As Morgan, Brian, Tyson and Rachel moved into Year 9 they had three opportunities to sustain and develop their identities as student teachers. They were challenged to become teachers of teachers as they taught their special skills to a group of 24 trainee Music teachers, then to a Year 7 class in another secondary school and finally to a Year 1 and 2 class in a primary school. Here we focus on the session with the younger pupils.

The class teacher's written reflections gave a sense of how the teaching episode developed and confirmed the student teachers' capacity to inform the professional knowledge of teachers. Here are several extracts from her notes which indicate how prepared she was to learn from the Y9 students. (Morgan, sadly, was ill and unable to be there.)

> I am always a little anxious when working in the hall [...] as the children appear to be more difficult to keep on task. The beginning of the lesson was delivered by Rachel and they stayed on task during Brian and Tyson's dance. The children were engaged from the outset. Rachel worked very quietly with the group of girls and mostly modelled the dance moves using very little verbal communication. It occurred to me that I should spend more time modelling moves during PE rather than explaining verbally as it appeared the girls were finding it easier to follow the visual instructions. Many of the children had smiles on their faces, particularly a little girl in Y2 whom I would describe as a 'fairy-like' character; she had a broad grin across her face after she had practised the moves modelled by her student teacher. The children were watching her every move throughout; they worked on their moves with much concentration.

> The boys were invited to pair up. I normally pair the children up myself (into carpet buddies – which are mixed ability pairs). I was surprised about some of the mixes but the children all worked very well in these pairs. A few of the boys are a little like puppies and if they are given too much leeway they can become very excitable and difficult to get back on track. But this wasn't the

case. The children were digesting what they had been shown and trialling each move, building up to the final dance moves. I feel I encourage the children to express themselves verbally but I don't give them the freedom to move freely [but] Tyson and Brian gave the children the time and freedom to experiment and feel comfortable with their dance moves. Therefore, when the children 'appear' to be off task in a physical lesson, perhaps I should stand back for a little longer.

During the time the children experimented with their moves one of the children stood stock still in the middle of the group. At this point, I would have gently reminded him to concentrate and continue working. However, Tyson and Brian left him to stand for a few minutes. He then returned to his partner and continued to work. Was he taking in information from what his peers were doing? Do I give him adequate opportunity to do this? Does he need the stimulus from his peers? Did Tyson and Brian intentionally give him a chance to take time out?

Also, during this time of experimentation another boy, who has severe dyspraxic tendencies and problems with concentration, took himself to one side of the hall and held onto the hanging ropes watching the other children. Did he need this time out because of sensory overload? Does he need time out to physically recuperate? Was he taking information from the other children? Do I give him enough time out? Were Tyson and Brian respecting that he needed this time out?

One of the boys has a particular problem coping with the environment of the hall. He can react by becoming rather wild and buzzing around the hall like a trapped bee. During these times it is very difficult to communicate with him as he seems to be trapped in his own world of excitement. He can also react to new situations by becoming extremely frightened and the colour in his face will drain away and he will try to explain that he 'doesn't like it.' When he is under stress I ask him whether he wants to sit on the bench and have a break and return to the group when he is ready. I gauge when this is and bring him back to the group. I don't know what had happened but during the lesson Tyson was sitting on a bench talking to him …. [He] spoke to him for some time. The child was sitting with his back slightly toward Tyson and his face was slightly drawn. Tyson was amazingly patient, caring and calming. He handled the situation with great sensitivity. The child returned to the group and continued with the lesson.

I was very impressed that the student teachers pitched their lesson to the correct level of the ability of the children in their charge. They had a fantastic rapport with the children; they were not trying to be pals with the children and as such commanded respect.

The most surprising part of the whole teaching was when the student teachers presented the children with certificates. I had observed very closely the student teachers with the children and throughout they seemed to effortlessly teach but didn't appear to be assessing the children. However, during the certificate-giving, I was amazed to find that they had been assessing and their assessment of the children was very insightful. They presented one boy with a certificate for being the most confident boy. One boy was presented with a certificate for taking part even though he didn't want to – again, very well assessed. The last presentation was to a boy for being the best dancer. This was interesting because many of the children in this class have private dance and Music lessons but this boy doesn't. However, I would say that he is the most naturally musical boy in the class.

I left this lesson with many questions about my own teaching and teacher training. Rachel, Tyson and Brian proved themselves as very intuitive teachers. Every child achieved the lesson objectives and enjoyed themselves too. There was truly excellence and enjoyment.

Such opportunities had enabled the students to harness their insights and talents in acts that were constructive for their own learning as well as for the learning of others.

In the next section, we shall see how difficult it was, in their own schools, for teachers to recognise the changes in them. As Brian had said (see page 70) somewhat resentfully, 'They haven't noticed I'm different.'

Risks, achievements and challenges

'Gifted pupils get chance to teach' was the headline in the Leadership section of the *Times Educational Supplement* in June 2004; William Stewart's report told how 'a school is making the most of its young stars by allowing them to teach PE'. The scheme is building pupils' confidence, he said, 'It gave the pupils a chance to shine.' The students involved were in the final years of secondary school and described as 'elite athletes' with specialist understanding of their sports and holding coaching awards. 'The London Gifted and Talented', a Government-funded agency supporting the work, believes that the initiative could be transferred across schools and to other subjects – in particular to the arts.

The initiative illustrates a growing understanding that students are capable of becoming active agents in the learning process and that schools are places capable of redefining child–adult relationships. Confidence and self-esteem grow and attitudes to learning change through the challenge of becoming mentors and teachers. By recognising students' leadership potential, acknowledging their level of social maturity, change can be triggered and schools can improve.

The basic premise of the project described in this book supports this conviction, but we venture in a different direction, for the notion of leadership in the PE scheme gave the successful a chance to shine. The 11 students in our project were not among the successful and were unlikely, in conventional terms, ever to be so.

Despite being in the early years of secondary school, their disaffection with school had been acknowledged by many of their teachers. Unlike the elite athletes described above, our students possess talents largely unrecognised by their schools, talents that form crucial aspects of their identity and potential. By ignoring these talents, opportunities to represent the whole child and to connect with their sources of self-expression, creativity, agency and autonomy are lost. These dimensions, we maintain, lie at the heart of an education in and through the arts. Institutional denial of them is likely to contribute to a sense of alienation from schooling.

The 11 students are easily labelled in negative terms, variously viewed as 'defensive, rude, challenging, argumentative, confrontational, withdrawn, unfocused, difficult, having attitude, without ambition, lacking in confidence and slow to take responsibility'. The list could be extended. Some have high status amongst their peers and their self-esteem is built on a reputation for being difficult in class; they have negative leadership qualities. Others exist on the margins or as outsiders. The young people involved in each of the four projects were challenging and as such had been trusted with little agency or responsibility:

> It demands imaginative action many times for teachers to realise that youngsters who see different have something to say about the way things might be if they were otherwise. **–Greene, 1995**

The project opened up a number of risks for the students involved. They were asked to see the school through different eyes and this involved a revision of boundaries among all those involved, the student teachers, the group taught, the classroom teachers and ourselves the onlookers. The students, by being accorded the status of teachers and thus experts in their fields, were both collaborators and leaders in the research. Although vastly experienced as recipients of the practice of teaching, in claiming the role of teacher for themselves, a new set of responsibilities confronted them. This promised to provide a source of intense personal learning.

There was risk too in moving beyond the well-documented and much rehearsed safer leadership roles given to students. They were to become more than prefects and monitors. In placing them in the role of teachers, asked to select and define subject knowledge and skills in their own terms and to design their own sequence of learning, they were given greater challenge. In this they had opportunity to exercise real power and to redefine power relationships. These students were well aware of how power operated within their schools. Participation in such a project could jeopardise the only source of power they had, the respect of their peers, because this respect was based largely on maintaining an oppositional stance.

The challenge, then, lay in being socialised into the norms of their school: becoming openly committed to its agenda, taking on a teacher's role, caring about something in school, abandoning the persona they adopted for their peers. In the past, they had not felt that they had a genuine stake in their school's teaching and learning, neither its content nor its processes, and they had not been judged reliable enough to be given real responsibilities. Unsurprisingly, they started with little confidence in being able to contribute to anything in school. The project posed huge personal risk for our students – there was a very real possibility that their ideas might not work.

As one teacher put it (see page 19):

> *If you start to care about something, that's actually quite dangerous. Because if you start to care how well you do, say at school, then if you fail it matters. Whereas if you spend all your time saying, 'I don't care' then if you fail it doesn't matter.*

It is easy in the current educational climate to seek simple definitions, outcomes and answers. Did we re-engage the disengaged? Is there a simple repeatable formula that we can apply in all contexts with all students? Not so easy to answer. Yet there are enough connections and common experiences across the stories to provide valuable insights into ways in which students might be re-engaged through the arts. The students' response to the challenge was impressive. Central to their challenge was the call to analyse the process of teaching and learning and to test their ideas about the conditions that bring about students' engagement and learning. These students may well, in the past, have used their insights as a basis for avoiding learning. They have much that is important to tell us about making learning better.

Pedagogical insight

> *Some teachers will just stand in front of a class and think, 'It's my right to teach you, you have to sit there and shut up.' You know what? That's not going to work with kids, not these kids.* –**Head of year**

Work on consulting students about teaching and learning has shown that they are indeed observant, analytical and constructive, rarely oppositional and frequently insightful. Their capacity to analyse social situations and in particular the quality of human interaction is sophisticated. In the extensive range of interviews with students carried out in two earlier projects (see Rudduck et al, 1996; Rudduck and Flutter, 2004) five themes emerged as important: students looked for security, respect-with-fairness, challenge-with-support, responsibility and autonomy. Most significant amongst these was autonomy. For students, this meant having an opportunity to make decisions about their learning and to have scope for active, problem-solving work on real issues. Beyond this, students wanted to be trusted to help others with their learning and to have control over their own progress in learning. The challenge presented to the students in the present project reflected this agenda. Their knowledge of pedagogy and their visions of what would constitute optimal learning conditions were critical factors in the success of the teaching episodes. Their skilful approach to engaging their learners underlined this capacity for good pedagogic practice.

The six boys and five girls took trouble in their lesson planning to engage the learners in their charge. They considered carefully what would motivate, what was relevant and what was appropriate. They analysed lessons given by their best teachers and that they knew had worked. They evaluated strategies that their own teachers had successfully employed. They recognised the need to gain knowledge of the learners, to understand their prior learning, their interests and concerns, and recognised the necessity to consult them. They accepted the need to produce exemplary material and through this to make clear what would constitute quality and determine value. They demonstrated respect for the technical language of their subjects. They knew they would need to explain with care and question skilfully. They recognised the need for challenge coupled with scaffolded support and the importance of re-framing questions when necessary and adapting or clarifying aspects of the task. There was a good grasp of lesson structure. They showed absolute respect for their students, maintaining a personal space for each student in which to imagine and discover. They allowed their students to have ideas and to create a learning dialogue. They were quick to confirm the individual and group response. They expected collaborative engagement. They willingly reflected on their teaching and their learners' responses.

Their teachers noted 'best selves' in evidence. We recall that Lauren showed the kinder, more sensitive, warmer side of her personality and that Tyson and Brian were quick to identify with the one unwilling student, showing patience and concern. Ashley learned to care. It was common for them to work the way of Jason, 'with gentle authority and with a genuine empathy'. The students were quick to attend to those in most need and those who they themselves and the rest of their group might learn from. Their intentions were clear yet free from highly specified outcomes. They were willing to be surprised by the unexpected. Indeed, they knew little of what to expect. Nel Noddings speaks, importantly, of the need for students to engage with subject matter directly and to be free from 'the mediation supplied by precise objectives'. She urges that the subject matter be worth looking at and listening to, and that it can be played with, and she warns that it may respond unexpectedly (2003).

The students had to take responsibility for the learning of others and in the process became reflective practitioners. Maxine Greene (1995) highlights the significance of this shift of role for young people:

> ... they are pre-challenged to become active learners, not simply passive receivers of digested information. They are asked with increasing frequency to tell their stories, to pose their own questions.

The response of the younger learners was positive. Almost all students spoke positively about the experience. They valued the quality of relationships, the effective levels of communication and the friendly, supportive interactions.

The necessary conditions for learning identified through earlier research – security, respect-with-fairness, challenge-with-support, responsibility and autonomy – were met.

Changing perceptions

The 11 students were moved by their experience. The challenge had been tough and there had been much to lose. They were exhilarated by their success. There was pleasure that the students they had taught had responded well and confirmed them in their role. They had been given responsibility and shown that they were mature enough to use it well. The project had mattered to them. They had enjoyed the chance to get better at something and to achieve. There was nothing routine or dull about this experience of school. It was intrinsically worthwhile. 'It makes you feel like you've gave something to someone and you haven't received nothing back, besides like proudness and that'. This insight alone might lead to rethinking the nature of 'engagement'.

Beyond empathising with the young people they taught, they expressed fresh understanding about their teachers. They were quick to acknowledge how difficult it must be to be a teacher:

Some of them have the patience of a saint, no, they have.

[Teaching] five times a day, five days a week. That must be tough, harder than we appreciate.

I'm going to be good to my teachers from now on.

I feel I want to help my teachers more.

You can understand why our teachers get frustrated so easily.

The experience gave new confidence to some to talk to their teachers more easily and to develop a sense of fellowship. Being involved in the project brought a feeling of commitment. There was pride in having managed their responsibilities and they were beginning to see themselves differently:

My attitude in class has definitely improved.

Quite good to be having the power.

I felt more mature after I had done it.

We want to stick with this, see how far it could go.

Their teachers noted transformations in attitudes and in relationships with many of the student teachers:

- Graham seemed to have been rehabilitated.
- Mark's peers were looking up to him now.
- Lauren was doing her homework.
- Tyson was happier with himself.
- Kayleigh was working on a task with great enthusiasm.
- Kurt was attending school.
- Rachel was more confident in speaking.
- Brian was no longer one of the top 20 troublemakers in his year.
- Ashley was sharing her new-found reading habit with her peers.

As the Music teacher says, 'They seem to understand a lot more.'

Maxine Greene (1995) suggests that one of the most important goals we should have as educators is to enable students to take initiatives in the education process toward becoming reflective learners and ultimately practitioners. The students here became those 'practitioners' – they were active participants in their own learning, gaining meaningful control over their own school lives and were able to view significant others in a more positive light.

The schools' perceptions of the student teachers

Jean Rudduck (2001) reminds us that schools, in their deep structures and patterns of relationships, have changed less in the last 20 years or so than young people have changed and that school improvement is about creating a better match between school and young people. At the heart of this mismatch lies our outdated perceptions of young people. The responsibilities and challenges given to students in secondary school, particularly in the first few years, often fail to match the levels of agency and social maturity that are part of their reality beyond school. Out of school, many students know how to learn and access information through their mastery of new technologies, some will be experienced carers with demanding household responsibilities, some are skilled mediators in personal and social relationships and capable of acting as significant actors within complex social networks.

The picture within school is often different from this. Seen as immature and on a particular rung of the ladder, they are easily defined in terms of being 'got ready' for this and that – got ready to move to secondary school, got ready for tests – but seen as not yet ready to take responsibility, not yet ready to be given challenging tasks, not yet ready for freedom to choose. We often explain their lack of initiative or their helplessness as something emanating from the environment beyond school rather than something learned and compounded within school. This is precisely how Morgan, for example, was seen and yet she proved herself capable of teaching and supporting others in school – something she does every Friday evening as a majorette within her community.

Despite a range of images of childhood developed in modern times, one endures above all others: childhood as an age of dependency (Rudduck, 2003). We are preoccupied, says Ann Oakley (1994) with young people as 'becoming' – with their status as 'would-be' adults – rather than with the here and now state of 'being', and this perception can lead us to underestimate their present capabilities. The ideology of immaturity is still pervasive. And as Mike Wyness observes, 'In many contexts and for a variety of reasons, the child as a subordinate subject is a compelling conception. It is time to review our notions of childhood' (2000). Sustaining the kind of temporary changes experienced by the students in this study will largely depend upon matching a re-envisaged schooling with the social realities of young people.

Curriculum and institutional constraints

Despite 20 years of reforming and adapting the curriculum in order to enable all students to show what they know, understand and can do, and despite repeated calls to recognise a wider range of student achievements, little has changed for a significant number of students. What counts as success continues to deny a broad range of personal attributes and capabilities. The expression, for example, of what one teacher involved in the project described as 'students' creative side' has little status on the ladder of success that is currently what counts. In the present climate, narrowly defined goals drive both teachers and students. Official doctrine, set in place with the establishment of a National Curriculum 16 years ago, silenced the basic need for self-expression and creativity. The subjective lives of young people, their search for greater knowledge of themselves – what they could do, who they might become, their need for self-esteem and personal meaning – have been overrun by a curriculum focused on forms of knowledge that are detached from the knower.

The result of a target-orientated model of education leads too often to what Seymour B Sarason calls 'passionless conformity' (1980). At the same time, a false dichotomy between a child-centered education and subject discipline has created some disorientation within arts education. There is little expectation that students themselves might be capable of contributing to a sharper definition of an education in and through the arts or even in assisting in its transformation.

The work of cognitive psychologist Howard Gardner has been taken up with enthusiasm in many schools where there is recognition that significant numbers of students are failing to access the curriculum offered. Gardner's theory of multiple intelligence breaks with unitary notions of intelligence where success is dependent upon a limited range of capabilities. Interpersonal and intra-personal intelligence, for example, are significant aspects of Gardner's theory (1993; 1999). Yet these have no currency within national measures of success on which a school and its teachers depend for survival, status and self-esteem. What Robin Tanner (1987) called the 'cramped conditions of our time' are difficult to transcend.

It is easy to fasten labels on students and we know that students believe they are impossible to remove. Their experience is that adult perceptions of them are continually reinforced and embedded in the collective memory. Beyond being forced to reconsider what constitutes good pedagogic practice, working with the 11 students in this project leads to a review of what might be possible for young people. The students here surprised themselves, the students they taught, their teachers and ourselves, the coordinators of the project. They had moved from casual non-concern, captured by Sarason (1990) in the lines below, to a stronger sense of membership of their school community:

> When one has no stake in the way things are, when one's needs or opinions are provided no forum, when one sees oneself as the object of unilateral actions, it takes no particular wisdom to suggest that one would rather be elsewhere.

The four schools we worked with welcomed involvement in the project, yet in most of them, competing agenda or established perceptions prevented what had been opened up from being developed. The Music teacher wished to share his project experience with senior management colleagues but found that there were challenges here that the school as a whole was not willing or ready to accept. There were different patterns of reluctance or avoidance or delay in other schools: in one, for instance, an imminent school inspection focused everyone's energy and there was little left for following through the project. Mark, despite his achievement in the project, had no say in determining his future contributions to school improvement and Jason became again an occupier of the school's isolation room for monitoring miscreants.

Richard Hickman, reflecting upon the project within one school, wrote:

> *I felt slightly uncomfortable with the notion of taking someone with challenging behaviour and manipulating circumstances so that the challenging behaviour is channelled into something 'positive', ie socialisation into the accepted norms of the institution. I tend to think that if I were in Jason or Mark's situation, I too would want to challenge the authority of the school.*

These concerns echo those of Helen Colley in her book, *Mentoring for School Inclusion* (2003). She asks whether mentoring – in our case tutoring/teaching – is 'a form of empowerment' or 'a process of control' (p135). She also challenges (p28) initiatives that are designed primarily to enable 'young people to reinvent themselves' so that they fit the institution they are in. We saw the situation differently – it was about mutual adaptation: the project sought to provide opportunities whereby schools might see and build on the talents of students who were not finding it easy to work to their strengths in school, and might change, in particular, the labelling system which 'fixes' reputations and prevents young people from trying out alternative identities as learners. As Ashley had said (see page 20): 'I've like this reputation hanging over me and I don't really want it. I want to be looked at as me not just my reputation.' The recognition and respect that the student teachers experienced allowed them to cast off their negative reputations – at least in some of their classes.

Richard Hickman also said:

> *Schools may espouse democracy and egalitarian ideals, but many are at best benignly authoritarian and are essentially hierarchical. Students being given a voice will do nothing to change this unless there are changes in attitude on the part of those in authority and in the structures and systems currently in place.*

In another school, Lauren's day of glory in the classroom was followed by more detentions, although fewer than she had been given before she became involved in the project. The potential was slipping away because of the pressure schools were under to give attention to other things. The irony speaks loudly.

Re-engaging the disengaged

A number of issues emerged during the project that need to be addressed if we are to be successful in re-engaging the disengaged. Although in this book, the framework was the arts – Drama, Design and Technology, Art and Design and Music – the approach could work well with different curriculum frames: PE (as we saw in the opening of Chapter 7), creative writing or History, and virtually any other. What matters is the principle of finding something that the disengaged are interested in, have some talent in and that can be linked to the formal curriculum.

There are some questions that schools should think about if they want to develop the kind of work described in this book:

1 Disengagement can be a cause and also an outcome of many behaviours that can justifiably be termed 'difficult':

   • *What do you know about the things that lead students to disengage? Are these highly individual or is there a more common pattern?*

   • *What strategies are presently used in school to help the disengaged to re-engage? How effective are they?*

2 It is difficult for students to change a negative label; it requires changes of perception on the part of teachers:

   • *How can we convince students that change is possible?*

   • *How can we develop a culture in schools that sees such change as possible?*

3 The task of supporting students in the process of change is not easy and seems to depend in part on rebuilding students' self-esteem, convincing them that they matter in school, helping them to redirect negative energy, and fostering positive behaviours:

   • *How can teachers build into the curriculum opportunities for students to share the talents that they have with others?*

   • *In what ways can disengaged students be given responsibilities that allow them to contribute meaningfully to the work of the school?*

   • *How can achievement, outside that which is valued and assessed within the curriculum, be acknowledged?*

4   We may need to acknowledge the emotional vulnerability of disengaged students:

> • *How can we look behind negative behaviours to identify individual vulnerabilities and strengths?*
>
> • *How can opportunities to develop empathy for others be developed in schools?*

5   Disengaged students may enjoy the respect of their peers for behaviours that are anti-work and anti-school. The experience of peer teaching and/or mentoring is one way of rebuilding a different image in the eyes of fellow students and allows the disengaged to review their relationships with others and their attitude to school and to themselves as members of the school community:

> • *Can opportunities for peer leadership be set up in your school?*
>
> • *What other strategies might be manageable?*

6   Teachers can learn a great deal about what students see as good teaching practice – ie teaching that engages them and motivates them to work well – from listening to students' accounts of what helps them to learn and what switches them off:

> • *How do/can teachers in your school gain insight into what particular students or groups of students think about teaching and learning?*
>
> • *How can learning become a more collaborative process?*
>
> • *Should we be responding to students' requests that learning should be more 'real', 'more 'fun' and more 'theirs'?*
>
> • *How can we build more democratic relationships in the classroom which allow a more open exploration of problems and possible ways forward?*

7   Disaffected students can redirect negative energy into something more positive if they are given more, rather than less, responsibility and agency within the school system:

> • *What sorts of responsibility are likely to signal to the disengaged that they are trusted and can make contributions that the school values?*
>
> • *How easy is it for the 'alternative' talents of disengaged students to be recognised, developed and shared within the school context?*

References

Chaplain R (1996) Making a strategic withdrawal: disengagement and self-worth protection in male pupils, in Rudduck J, Chaplain R and Wallace G (eds) *School Improvement – What Can Pupils Tell Us?* (pp101–115), London: David Fulton

Colley H (2003) *Mentoring for Social Inclusion*, London: RoutledgeFalmer

Csikszentmihalyi M (1990) *Flow: The Psychology of Optimal Experience*, New York: Harper and Row

ERSC/TLRP Project (2003) *Consulting pupils about teaching and learning*, University of Cambridge Faculty of Education, Web site: www.consultingpupils.co.uk

Galton M, Gray J and Rudduck J et al (2003) *Progress in the Middle Years of Schooling (7–14): Continuities and Discontinuities in Learning*, Final Report to the DfES

Gardner H (1993) *Frames of Mind: The Theory of Multiple Intelligence*, London: Fontana

Gardner H (1999) *Intelligence Reframed*, New York: Basic Books

Greene M (1995) *Releasing the Imagination: Essays on Education, the Arts, and Social Change*, San Francisco: Jossey-Bass

Harland J, Kinder K, Kord P, Stott A, Schagen I, Haynes J et al (2000) *Arts Education in Secondary Schools: Effects and Effectiveness*, Slough, NFER

Morrison I, Everton T and Rudduck J (2000) Pupils helping other pupils with their learning, *Mentoring and Tutoring*, 8, 3, 187–200

Noddings N (2003) *Happiness and Education*, Cambridge: Cambridge University Press

Oakley A (1994) Women and children first and last, in B Mayall (ed) *Children's Childhoods: Observed and Experienced*, London: Falmer Press

Rudduck J (2001) Students and school improvement: 'Transcending the cramped conditions of the time', *Improving Schools*, 4, 2, 7–16

Rudduck J (2003) The transformative potential of consulting young people about teaching, learning and schooling, *Scottish Educational Review*, 34, 2, 123–137

Rudduck J, Chaplain R and Wallace G (eds) (1996) *School Improvement: What Can Pupils Tell Us?*, London: David Fulton

Rudduck J and Flutter J (2004) *How to Improve Your School: Giving Pupils a Voice*, London: Continuum

Sarason S (1990) *The Predictable Failure of Educational Reform*, San Francisco: Jossey-Bass

Shultz J and Cook-Sather A (2001) *In Our Own Words: Students' Perspectives on School*, New York: Rowan and Littlefield

Stewart W (2004) 'Gifted pupils get chance to teach', *Times Educational Supplement*, June 25, p10

Tanner R (1987) *Double Harness*, London: Impact Books

Willis P (1992) *Moving Culture: An Enquiry into the Cultural Activities of Young People*, London: Calouste Gulbenkian Foundation

Wyness M W (2000) *Contesting Childhood*, London: Falmer Press